Pathways to HOPE AND HEALING

Pathways to HOPE AND HEALING

Healing the Lasting Effects of Prolonged Stress, Trauma and Dysfunction

MILLIE MCCARTY, M.A., LPCC-S

Charleston, SC
www.PalmettoPublishing.com

Pathways to Hope and Healing

Copyright © 2023 by Millie McCarty, M.A., LPCC-S

No portion of this book may be reproduced, stored in a retrieval system, or transmitted in any form by any means—electronic, mechanical, photocopy, recording, or other—except for brief quotations in printed reviews, without prior permission of the author.

Requests for information should be addressed to:
The Healing Hub at the Gate
Pickerington, Ohio 43147
milliehealinghub4u@gmail.com

First Edition

Paperback ISBN: 978-1-7354796-1-3
eBook ISBN: 979-8-8229-1164-2

Millie McCarty, M.A., LPCC-S—Graduating Cum Laude from Defiance College with a B. A. Degree in Religious Education, Millie went on to receive her M.A. degree in Guidance and Counseling from The Ohio State University in 1981 and became a Licensed Professional Clinical Counselor in 1985. Millie's background as a Director of Education at her church and a Parenting Educator as well as a Personal Growth & Development Trainer added to the richness of her knowledge and ability to meet people where their need was.

Widely known in Ohio as a counselor and teacher, Millie served 20 years as the founder and Executive Director of Lighthouse Counseling Services from 1981—2001, when she retired to write and teach. Her groundbreaking work in the areas of early childhood sexual, ritual abuse, and dissociative identity disorder, has brought healing and restoration through her strategic, systematic design combining faith principles and proven professional strategies to thousands of adult victims of childhood sexual trauma to citizens of Ohio.

After retiring, Millie began a ten-year journey of co-writing a case study entitled "*RUTH: Secret of the Silenced Voices;*"—*A Guide to Working with People with Dissociative Identity Disorders.*" During this period from 2002–2012, as a by-product of the case study, Millie wrote her next book "*WHY WE CAN'T Just Get Over It*"—*Healing the Effects of Prolonged Stress and Trauma*. At the same time, developing her *"Systematic Process"* of resolving unresolved conflicts needed for restoration. Millie began being asked to train people from other nations such as China, Ethiopia, Jamaica, Finland, Haiti, Rwanda, Uganda, and Cuba. Today she is being called to train church leaders at home and abroad in her *Systematic Process* to equip the church for the great harvest that lies before us.

Systematic Process for Resolving Unresolved Conflict Eternally (SPRUCE)

From 2012–2017 Millie implemented a systematic approach to equipping others with the tools to provide care for survivors of abuse and trauma using her curriculum and implementing other coursework to provide the necessary skills to restore the life skills missed during the time of abuse and trauma. Based on her 35 years of counseling and training, these classes were established as a certification program. Her ultimate goal is to get the curriculum accredited and published to provide all nations with this *Systematic Process of Resolving Unresolved Conflict Eternal (SPRUCE)*.

This **HEALING THE HEART** course was designed specifically to take to the nations. It contains excerpts from "PATHWAYS TO HOPE AND HEALING," Copyright©2002 and "WHY WE CAN'T "JUST GET OVER IT", Copyright ©2009, both written by Millie McCarty, M.A., LPCC. All rights reserved. No part of this publication may be reproduced, transmitted in any form, or stored in a retrieval system without prior written permission of the author, except in the case of brief quotations embodied in articles and previews. Requests for information should be addressed to (e-mail: milliehealinghub4u@gmail.com).

CONTENT AND GOALS: Healing the Heart is a composite of both books developed by founder and CEO, Millie McCarty, MA., LPCC-Supervisor; "Pathways to Hope and Healing" and "Why We Can't Just Get Over It". To bring the core teachings of *INTERNATIONAL INSTITUTE FOR TRAUMA RECOVERY* ministry, we have chosen the most important sections of these two books to accomplish the following goals:

- To train participants in (Millie's) systematic approach to healing survivors of abuse and trauma using Millie McCarty's unique **SPRUCE** process, a *Systematic Process for Resolving Unresolved Conflict Eternally*
- To help participants apply the Biblical principles of healing to their trauma-based thoughts, emotions, and actions.
- To begin to understand the amazing neurological connection between the brain and gut and the power of our thoughts over our body's system that is designed to protect us; and how to begin to direct that energy and power in such a way that it brings healing instead of disease.
- To train participants in the systematic use of eight assessment tools that assist in getting to the root issues beneath the surface of the mental, emotional, and behavioral signs of stress and trauma. Once the roots have been uncovered, we learn how to do "Spiritual Surgery" to literally "take the ax to the root" … rooting out the lies and replacing them with God's Truth…. thus, facilitating their healing from trauma.

Why We Can't Just Get Over It was written as a result of a ten-year assignment to write a Case Study *RUTH: Secrets of the Silenced Voices*; the story of the life of one lady who had experienced a lifetime of abuse and trauma at the hands of her father's live-in friend who was a pedophile. Her life included every kind of abuse and torture including Satanic Ritual Abuse, yet, she went on to be functional as a schoolteacher and executive employee in the State Dept. of Social Services as well as maintaining a strong belief in God. Ruth lived to tell her story and assist Millie in teaching the first class of *RUTH* and *Why We Can't Just Get Over It* in China twice and Ethiopia before going home to her eternal peace in 2017.

Table of Contents

Preface	Purpose, Goals, and Note from Author, Author Biography	ix
Lesson One	Changing Times—Statistics, Biblical Model Vs. Medical Model	1
Lesson Two	Where the Battle Began—Generational Principalities	9
Lesson Three	Family Tree—Getting to The Root-Family System/Models	21
Lesson Four	Family Systems—Laying the Foundations	26
Lesson Five	Family Make a Difference—Four Types of Families	32
Lesson Six	Growing Up in Stages—Developmental Chart and Scars	37
Lesson Seven	Taking an Axe to The Root—Genogram	45
Lesson Eight	Walls We Build—Defense Mechanisms	57
Lesson Nine	Web of Lies—Types of Lies, God's Perception vs. My Perception	67
Lesson Ten	Lies, Oaths and Vows—Renouncing Oaths and Vows, Carrie's Story	74
Lesson Eleven	Out of Darkness—Cycle of Dysfunction and Illumination, Dan's Story	82
Lesson Twelve	Cycles of Addiction and Sin—Dying to Self	94
Lesson Thirteen	Building Healthy Boundaries—Safe and Unsafe Places	103
Lesson Fourteen	Breaking Free—Repentance, Forgiveness, Walking in The Spirit	110
Lesson Fifteen	Renewing the Mind—Mind Renewal, Changing Faulty Beliefs and Behaviors	122
Reference Notes		135
Personal Inventory Questionnaire		139
Other Books Written by Millie McCarty		147
Refrences List		149

Preface

PURPOSE:
- To provide an instrument of healing for people who struggle with a wide range of mental and emotional problems as a result of abuse and trauma resulting in physical, mental, emotional, neurological, and psychological problems—even spiritual problems—which lead to life choices involving drug and alcohol abuse and/or other methods of temporary coping that leads to dysfunction, disease, and death.
- To illuminate the root causes of mental, emotional, and behavioral problems to bring people out of darkness into the light.
- To provide a process by which people can replace their destructive beliefs and perceptions that lead to compulsive, addictive, or destructive consequences.

GOALS:
- To experience the integration of biblical and professional principles in healing
- To use tools that identify the roots of mental, physical, and emotional problems
- To identify ways in which faulty beliefs systems affect mental, emotional, and physical well-being
- To Identify qualities of safe people and places
- To recognize the effects of trauma and developmental issues
- To identify processes to rebuild one's life
- To identify steps of our biblically based ILLUMINATION healing process

"For though we walk in the flesh, we do not war after the flesh: (For the weapons of our warfare are not carnal, but mighty through God to the pulling down of strong holds;) Casting down imaginations, and every high thing that exalteth itself against the knowledge of God, and bringing into captivity every thought to the obedience of Christ; And having in a readiness to revenge all disobedience, when your obedience is fulfilled." —2 Corinthians 10:3-6

WHAT YOU WILL LEARN:
The content of this book is a training program developed to not only bring hope and healing to survivors of abuse and trauma but for training others to use this systematic approach to healing. This workbook has been developed for survivors of abuse and trauma of all kinds. Most survivors of abuse are silenced either by their abuser or by their shame and guilt. This shame and guilt may be assigned either by the offender who threatens to hurt them or a loved one if they tell or by themselves because their conscience tells them "This is good/right."

You will discover through these lessons that keeping things inside can cause deeper mental, emotional, and physiological damage as well as the destruction of our ability to care for ourselves and others. We will experience ways of exposing the truth to heal and restore your God-given identity.

Within this workbook, you may experience the following:
- Exposure to the truths of God's Word that have been hidden by the darkness.
- Open windows to the soul revealing hidden roots that lead to unhealthy emotions and destructive behavior.
- Tools to help identify patterns, cycles, and behaviors that need healing.
- Exercises to help identify events that affected human growth and development resulting in life-long problems.
- The power of the Word of God to shed light, and bring revelation and healing.
- The power of repentance and forgiveness to heal.
- The power to break generational curses that destroy lives.

"When I kept silent, my bones waxed old through my roaring all the day long. For day and night, thy hand was heavy upon me: my moisture is turned into the drought of summer. Selah. I acknowledged my sin unto thee, and mine iniquity have I not hid. I said, I will confess my transgressions unto the LORD; and thou forgavest the iniquity of my sin. Selah." —Psalm 32:3-5

NOTE FROM THE AUTHOR: My purpose in writing this book is to share with others what God has taught me as a Christian Educator, Parenting Instructor, and Professional Clinical Counselor through His Word. My professional concepts and practices uphold biblically based truth. These biblical and professional concepts have been used to train professional counselors, pastors, as well as non-professional caregivers to equip them for ministry to the broken and lost in their church and community. I believe this book can "open windows" to hurting souls through which God's light can shine to bring truth and healing; leading to changed lives.

Lesson One

CHANGING TIMES

Lesson One

Changing Times

Having grown up in the simplistic life of a small town in the mid-west, that peaceful existence couldn't prepare one for the culture shock of the sixties and seventies in a metropolitan city. Mobility separated people from their extended families. Technological changes and advances became a daily phenomenon giving the homemaker and mother more free time. Yet these changes forced many women into the workplace to be able to afford modern conveniences and thus, two cars were required so both adults could work. While separation from the extended family made raising children more difficult, post-war technological changes made us more independent and self-sufficient. By the sixties, post-war families owned their own homes, two cars, and all the amenities of the *All-American Life*.

In 1948 and 1953, a two-part "cultural phenomenon" took place with the publication of Dr. Alfred Kinsey's monumental works on male and female human sexuality (Sexual Behavior in the Human Male, Sexual Behavior in Human Female by Alfred C. Kinsey, Wardell B. Pomeroy, Clyde E. Martin and Paul H. Bebhard, W.B. Saunders, Philadelphia, 1953). The Kinsey Reports, more than any other documents in history, have shaped Western society's beliefs and understanding of human sexuality. Their impact on attitudes, subsequent developments in sexual behavior, politics, law, sex education, and even religion has been immense. However, the public does not generally realize this today (Kinsey, Sex, and Fraud, by Dr. Judith A. Reisman, Edward Eichel, Huntington House Publishers 1990).

The Vietnam War brought turmoil, rebellion, division, and strife to our land, pitting father and son, old and young against each other. Then the rebellion of the 1960s hit. Humanism began to undermine faith in the existence of God in a systematic progression.

The rebellion was not only about war but also about a mindset and a way of living. It became a war on our culture fed by secular humanism and slowly but methodically this rebellion indoctrinated our children through the schools with an anti-God, anti-establishment ideology that threatened to destroy the Judeo-Christian foundation of our lives.

By the 1970s, the validity of the Holy Bible, the bond of marriage, and the sanctity of life were negatively impacted by the decay of spiritual values. When the Liberation Movement swept our country, we were confronted with the whole God-is-dead movement that was an expression of rebellion against the Word of God and godly institutions such as church, marriage, family, and Christianity.

Widespread educational teaching of values clarification and situation ethics compounded the situation and Americans began walking the path of relativism, deceiving themselves about the importance of God's principles. Relativism was a renunciation of the existence of a Supreme Being and His laws to guide morality and meant doing whatever was right in our own eyes. In other words, the new law was "there is no absolute right and wrong".

THE EVOLUTION OF AMERICA

The foundation for this evolution was laid in the late 1870s. A new faith regarding law was introduced to America's educational system. The newly appointed Dean of Harvard Law School, Christopher Columbus Langdell, considered law to be an evolutionary science, consisting of certain principles or doctrines, which arrived at its present state by slow degrees. God's laws, which were irrevocable and eternal, were considered irrelevant. John Chipman Gray, a colleague of Langdell, said, "The law is a "living, changing thing with a continuous history, sloughing off the old, taking on the new." Langdell believed that man, led by the ablest scholars and judges, could discover and determine the laws governing human affairs. He believed that man didn't need the aid of God or the Holy Scripture, and therefore, sought to eliminate both from public education—not by default, but by design. He, along with the President of Harvard University, Charles W. Eliot, embraced the new faith that swept the academic world in the latter 1800s—that "Darwin's theory of evolution was the key to all life, including the law.

This new religion called Secular Humanism became "law" among educators and was introduced into the educational system in America. This led to a new definition of tolerance—a tolerance for everything BUT God and His laws, a tolerance for every faith BUT Christianity. Through this new teaching of tolerance and the rewriting of our history books, revisionists have made a major assault on the foundational teachings and governing principles that made America "the light of the world". By removing all signs of the faith of our founding fathers from our history books and changing laws to reflect paganism rather than Christianity, God's laws have become diluted with relativism. Prayer and biblical teachings are speedily being removed from our schools. The church has watered down its message so as not to "offend" any intolerance for God's Word and to make Christianity acceptable to the palette of secular America. With the Bible no longer undergirding our nation, Christian values and beliefs are assaulted and elements of secularism and paganism now dominate our music, literature, newspapers, and television. With the expansion of the media, expansive use of computers, and the internet, major inroads have been gained by presenting Christians as ignorant bumblers, criminals, and hypocrites who are "intolerant". God's laws regarding the sanctity of life, the sanctity of marriage, and the sanctity of sex are portrayed as archaic and irrelevant while paganistic values are lifted as "more tolerant" and acceptable. Tolerance no longer means "having respect for" different philosophies, but rather that all religions and philosophies are accepted EXCEPT God's laws and precepts. As a result, we have seen the breakdown of the American family through secular immorality.

SEX EDUCATION

Kinsey's report shook our nation and was instrumental in opening doors to the phenomenal growth of pornography—while sexually explicit magazines at every corner grocery store, sexual experimentation, and promiscuity spread among our teens. Sexual abuse and molestation as well as rape were on the increase. More and more movies promoted the values and claims of fraudulent statistics. The sex education of our colleges filtered down to include sex education in elementary schools and 70 years later efforts are being made to add sex education to the curriculum of our pre-schools.

All these changes were subtle and fast. So fast were changes being made, parents felt like they were watching the Indianapolis 500. No sooner was one value knocked down than a new opposing one emerged, not giving parents time to adjust to the first new cultural phenomenon before another one was added. And with all these changes came the growing drug culture and its effect on teen sex and violence. Multicultural changes were added as immigrants by the thousands (legally and illegally) entered our country without knowing the languages, customs, or laws of our nation. Thus, our nation became more lawless, and the traditional family couldn't find support from the government, community, or church. Families were not equipped to cope with the changes and the church was caught sleeping. Meanwhile, the government, without the balance of faith, was like a runaway train, zipping through city after city, destroying the infrastructure that once kept our country safe and strong.

FAMILY HOUSEHOLDS

Children are being neglected, abandoned, and abused due to broken homes and broken lives. According to a new Pew Research Center analysis of U.S. Census Bureau data, "The share of U.S. children living with an unmarried parent has more than doubled since 1968, jumping from 13% to 32% in 2017. That trend has been accompanied by a drop in the share of children living with two married parents, down from 85% in 1968 to 65% in 2017. Some 3% of children are not living with any parents."

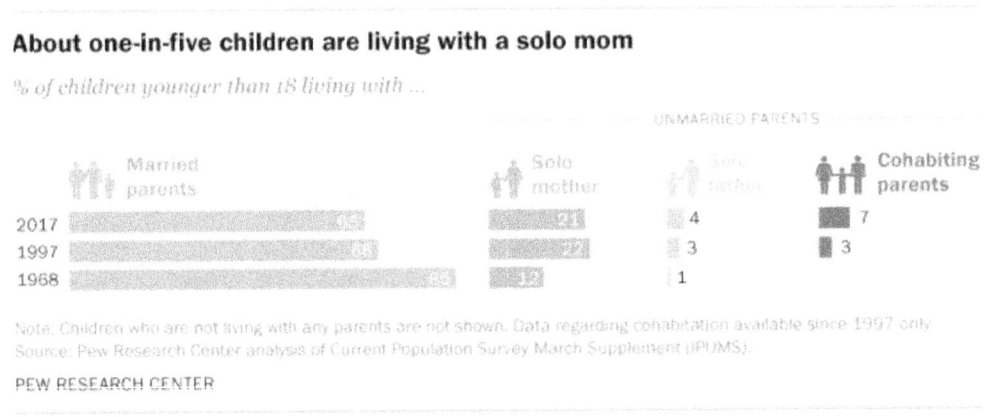

AFFECTS ON OUR CHILDREN

Children are neglected, abandoned, and abused due to broken families, divorce, and exposure to live-in partners. Children are having children, sometimes destroying them as soon as they are formed. The increased disintegration of families has also caused an increase in violence among children, teens, and adults as well as an increase in the number of children neglected, abused, and killed by parents.

Children from single-parent homes, especially those with no father influence, have directly resulted in the following:

- 75% increase in teen suicide by overdose
- Rising homicide rates for children
- Many rapists, murderers, and violent criminals (approximately 70% of adolescent murderers are from fatherless homes)
- Majority of the population in the criminal justice system (juvenile and adult)
- A continuing increase in arrests for violent crimes among minors
- An increase in the cost of operating the prison systems
- An increase in the number of drug-addicted babies
- An increase in drug and alcohol-related problems

- An increase in addiction to pornography
- An expansion of the AIDS epidemic
- Increase in sexual abuse of children, affecting their sexual identification
- Men and women growing up with an "orphan spirit".

ABORTION

It's estimated that nearly one million abortions take place annually and more than 55 million abortions have been performed in the U.S. since 1973, based on accumulative data from the two primary sources of U.S. abortion statistics—U.S. Centers for Disease Control (CDC) and the Guttmacher Institute.

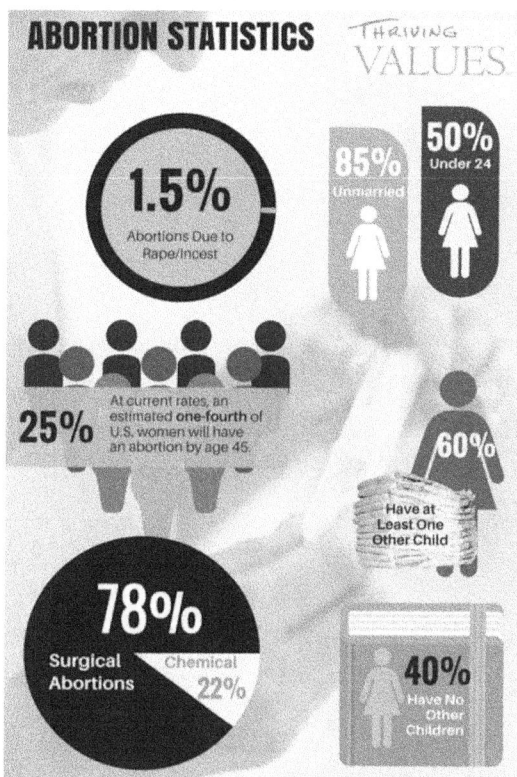

THE EPIDEMIC OF SUICIDE

Suicide is a leading cause of death in the United States. According to the Centers for Disease Control and Prevention (CDC) WISQARS Leading Causes of Death Reports, in 2016:
- Suicide was the tenth leading cause of death overall in the US, claiming the lives of nearly 45,000 people.
- Suicide was the second leading cause of death among individuals between the ages of 10 and 34, and the fourth leading cause of death among individuals between the ages of 35 and 54.
- There were more than twice as many suicides (44,965) in the US as there were homicides (19,362)

Past Year Suicidal Thoughts and Behaviors Among U.S. Adults (2017)
Data Courtesy of SAMHSA

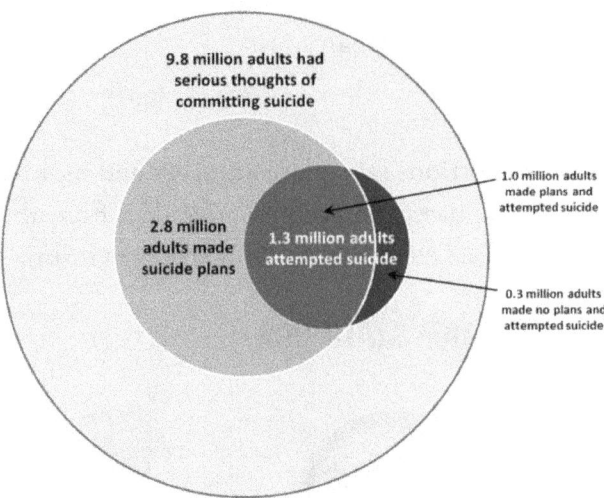

MENTAL HEALTH

Statistics show that one in five Americans experience a mental disorder in a year. Approximately 15% of all adults who have mental disorders in one year also experience co-occurring substance (alcohol or other drug) use disorder, which complicates treatment. 10% of the U.S. adult population uses mental health services in the health sector in any year, with another 5% seeking such services from social service agencies, schools, or religious or self-help groups. SAMHSA

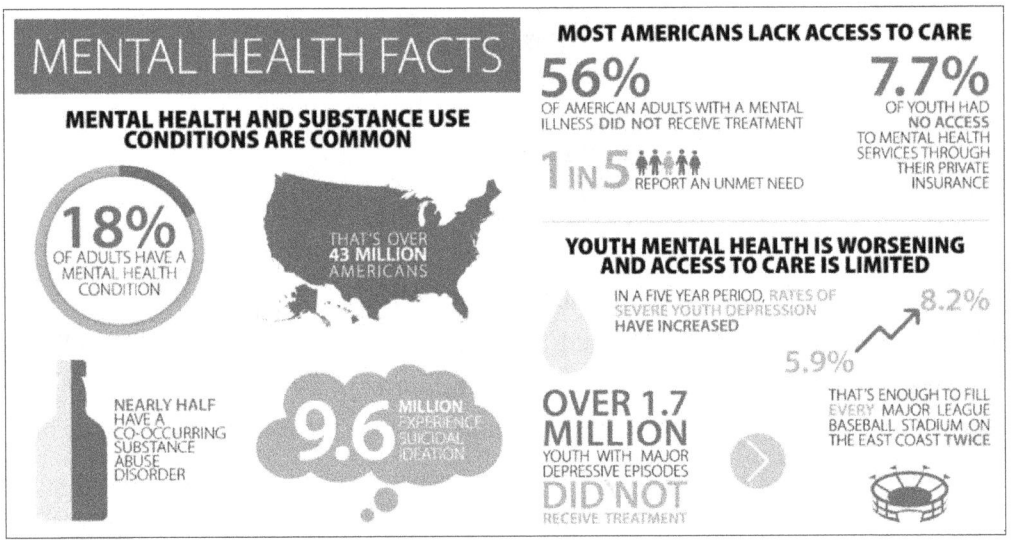

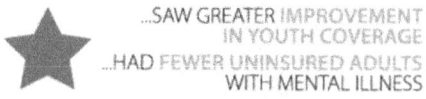

Mental Health of America

DRUG ABUSE AND ADDICTION

The National Institute on Drug Abuse reports over 20 million people nationwide suffer from drug and alcohol abuse issues. Perhaps worse, the cost of treatment and incarceration runs nearly $700 billion annually for taxpayers. It is also estimated that nearly 4.3 million Americans use prescription medications for non-medical reasons monthly. This abuse of drugs is now the number one cause of accidental death in the U.S.

PORNOGRAPHY

We live in a day and age when pornography is both more widely accessible and more widely accepted than ever before in history. The invention and ensuing commercialization of the internet nearly twenty years ago has brought with it one of the most widespread and seemingly inconspicuous epidemics that mankind has ever seen. Nowadays, men and women can simply open their laptops or turn on their TVs and in seconds have access to thousands of pornographic images and videos of forms: softcore, hardcore bestiality child porn—anything that suits their fancy. Just take a look at the shocking statistics on pornography given by UnitedFamilies.org:

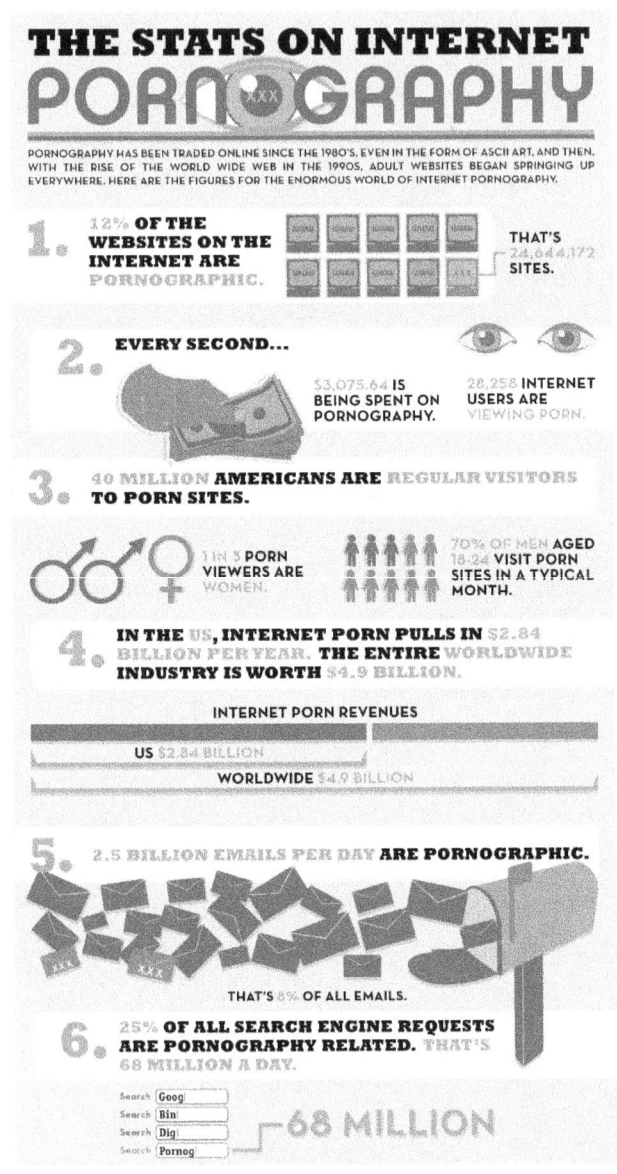
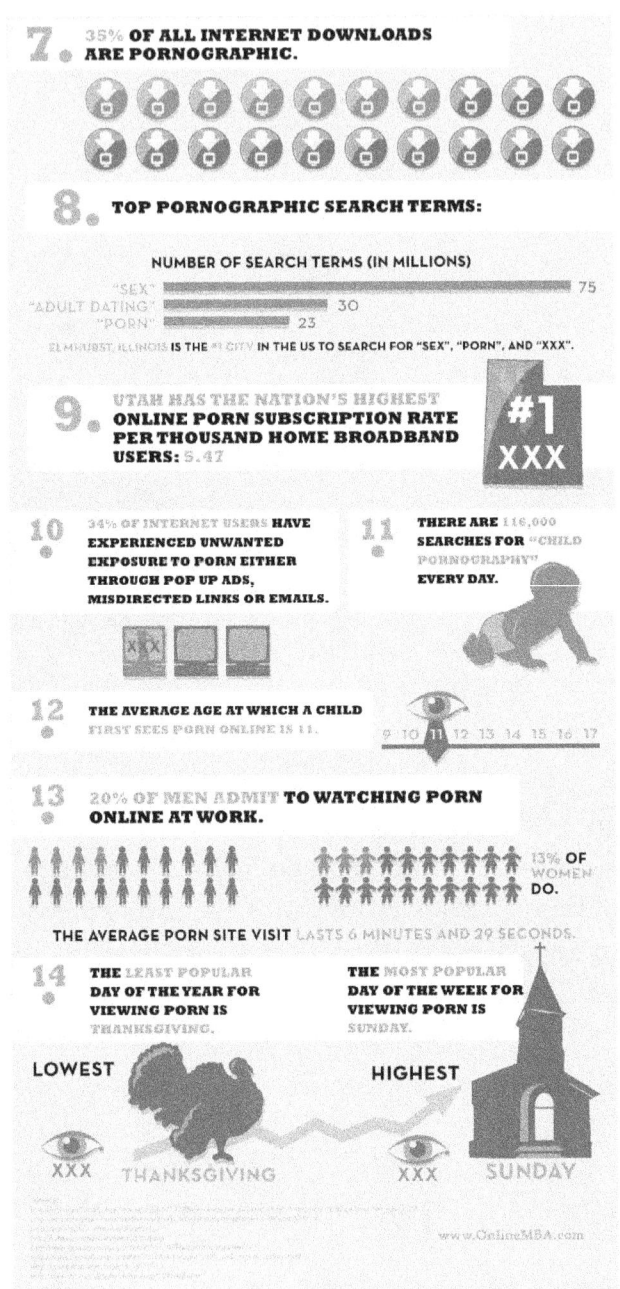

Lesson Two

Where the Battle Began

Lesson Two

Where the Battle Began

"And of some have compassion, making a difference: And others save with fear, pulling them out of the fire; hating even the garment spotted by the flesh" —Jude 1:22-23

The whole realm of authority was challenged in the 1960s. Even the Word was challenged as the true Word of God. To bring order out of our chaos, we must again understand God's principles based upon His Word. When we take back our authority, the world will begin to see the Church in a whole new way.

Without knowledge of God's Word, we can't discern right from wrong. As we discipline ourselves in the Word and exercise the Holy Spirit, we will see the reality of Christ in the days ahead. Today, too many Christians are walking in lies and deception, thus, weakening the church at large.

Our greatest fear is that we will upset someone with our beliefs. The anti-Christ spirit in our world today is challenging Christians to come forward. We will be further tested as we move into these coming days of ideological wars

It is said today that the church is becoming more and more like the world. This is the enemy's strategy. He loves to find places in our human nature where he can ensnare us to do his will. To prevent this, Christians must be in the world but not "of this world" —John 8:23. As we fellowship with believers and study God's Word, we recognize the guidance God provides for our preparation so, He can send us forth into the world without being trapped by the god of mammon (money).

We need the armor of God, prayer, and discipline. We also need to live the Word. This is also our equipping. God has provided everything we need to care for one another and to live our lives in such a way as to reap the blessings God has for His people.

"1 Now these are the commandments, the statutes, and the judgments, which the LORD your God commanded to teach you, that ye might do them in the land whither ye go to possess it: That thou mightest fear the LORD thy God, to keep all his statutes and his commandments, which I command thee, thou, and thy son, and thy son's son, all the days of thy life; and that thy days may be prolonged. —Deuteronomy 6:1-2

We must link together with believers of the truth so we can help each other discern the deceptions that attempt to undermine God's purposes. Standing on God's word, His wisdom will unlock the doors to victory over demonic forces that are rising against the church today. *Yes, we are our brother's keepers!* Jeremiah, an Old Testament prophet, who was a godly man walking in righteousness, was beaten and thrown in jail, then nearly starved before he was thrown into a cistern of mud. He was hated by people, who didn't want to hear the Word of God. It was a eunuch who saved him—a man rejected, shamed, humiliated, judged, ridiculed, and emasculated. His identity was stripped from him. He was a man of no worth to his society, yet God redeemed his life and placed him in the king's palace. When the eunuch saw Jeremiah in the pit, he knew what it was like to be humiliated and rejected, shunned and spat upon. The eunuch gathered a rope and rags to cushion Jeremiah's arms and pulled him up out of the pit.

Those who are like eunuchs in our time, who have been through the agonies of abuse, sickness, war, conflict, false accusation, and other violent and unfair treatment at the hands of others, are those who will have compassion—those who have faced death and been redeemed by the King of kings. The throwaways, the quiet, persevering servants of God, are the ones who will bring our nation out of the pit of darkness into the light of Christ. It is through their suffering that they developed the compassion and the strength to persevere and the power of the Holy Spirit to rise above the ways of the world to conquer evil.

> *"We are faced with continual change, conflict, fear, war, rumors of war, generations battling generations and generations battling among themselves."*

The enemy has many spirits that he sends out into the world to trap and trick humankind. God's people aren't immune to these strategies. There are spirits assigned to families, communities, territories, and nations. The biblical model describes people groups and how their actions and/or attitudes identified certain principalities that reigned over their lives.

> *"When the LORD thy God shall bring thee into the land whither thou goest to possess it, and hath cast out many nations before thee, the Hittites, and the Girgashites, and the Amorites, and the Canaanites, and the Perizzites, and the Hivites, and the Jebusites, seven nations greater and mightier than thou; And when the LORD thy God shall deliver them before thee; thou shalt smite them, and utterly destroy them; thou shalt make no covenant with them, nor shew mercy unto them: Neither shalt thou make marriages with them; thy daughter thou shalt not give unto his son, nor his daughter shalt thou take unto thy son. For they will turn away thy son from following me, that they may serve other gods: so, will the anger of the LORD be kindled against you, and destroy thee suddenly."* —Deuteronomy 7:1-4

PRINCIPALITIES OVER FAMILIES AND NATIONS

"For we wrestle not against flesh and blood, but against principalities, against powers, against the rulers of the darkness of this world, against spiritual wickedness in high places." —Ephesians 6:12

Each of the nations mentioned had demonic spirits that characterized these groups of people:

Hivites: Were known for discrediting and slander; repeating matters outside of proper channels of authority and relations and tale-bearing. (I Peter 4:15)

Perizzites: Were known for division and contention, setting up ambushes to cause fighting against each other. (Matthew 12:25)

Jebusites: Were known for their filth, uncleanness, and sexual immorality.
(II Peter 2:9-10, Romans 6:18-20, I Thessalonians 4:3-7)

Amorites: Were prideful, arrogant, self-centered, unteachable, and delighted in finding defects in leadership. (Numbers 21:13, Psalms 73:6-9, Proverbs 8:13, Proverbs 16:18, Proverbs 29.22).

Girgashites: Were a people known for anxiety and worry—a basic distrust of God and unbelief. (Hebrews 3:19) Their cares are choked because of their lack of trust in God. (Matthew 13:22)

Hittites: Were known for their discouragement, complaining, and murmuring, which brings on depression and despondency. (Moses: Numbers 11:10-15), (Elijah: 1 King 19:1-9), (Disciples: John 6:58-60)

Canaanites: Were known for their superiority; making people feel inferior, paranoid, fearful, overwhelmed, intimidated, and rejected. (Numbers 13:33)

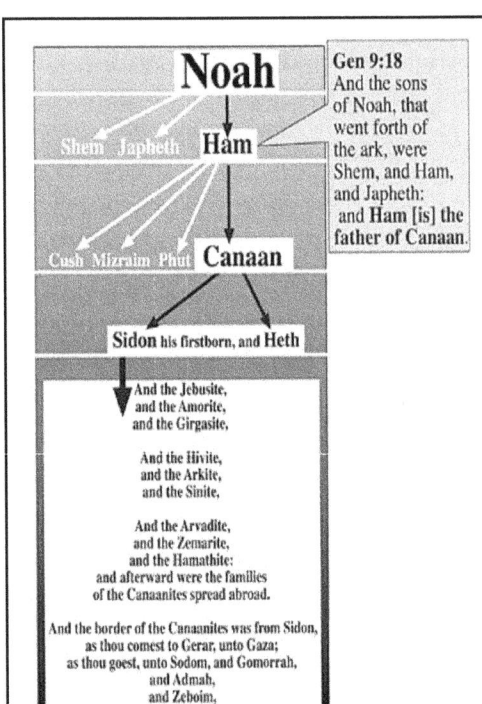

The descendants of Canaan were some of the most wicked people to ever live on the earth—the people of Sodom and Gomorrah for instance. It is indeed possible that Noah saw in Canaan the same sin problem that his father Lamech had. When the father sins, the next generation learns from the father and are often more wicked than their father.

Therefore, it seems that Noah's descendants would also reflect this rebellious nature. Remember, the people of Sodom and Gomorrah were judged for their sexual perversion.

The curse of Canaan is in fact an example warning fathers to train their children in godly principles. If this is not done in one generation, then generations to come will express their rebellious nature as seen in the wickedness of Canaan's descendants.

Commentary made available by
http://www.answersingenesis.org/creation/v20/i3/china.asp
COPYRIGHT © 2005 Answers in Genesis

REFLECTIVE EXERCISE

Have your students make note of the above characteristics and see how many they recognize that are active in their family, school, modeled in media, and people around you. After roleplaying the above qualities and behaviors of these principalities, discuss the following questions:

1. How do these actions/behaviors influence your thinking and behavior?

2. How does God's Word direct us to know and discern right from wrong?

3. How can we separate ourselves from the ways of the world?

4. Identify the major battles being waged today between forces of good and evil.

You are recognizing how God is restoring the body of Christ and empowering us through the Holy Spirit to be healers and restorers. What are your ideas on some suggested ways that the Church should rise and be the "light" that Christ intended it to be?

Examine your own life considering the attitudes and behaviors we have discussed regarding the "ites." Identify the attitudes and behaviors in your own life that are present in the lives of the "ites." These are learned and modeled by the world around you, but you have a choice to walk in the light of God's light; experiencing much more love, joy, and peace in your life.

Make note of how many of the principality characteristics you recognize in your family, community, business, school, media, and people around you. How do they influence your thinking and behavior?

_____
_____
_____
_____

Choose one negative behavior or action you recognize in your own life that you want to change and commit to working on in the coming weeks.

_____
_____
_____
_____

Meditate on the following characteristics of a warrior that can help you overcome the influences of your culture. Rate yourself on a score of 1–10 (1= lowest and 10 = highest):

____ Confidence in knowing you belong to God   ____ Steadfastness
____ Faith in God's Word   ____ Sobriety
____ Good conscience   ____ Endurance
____ Earnestness   ____ Self-Denial

If you aren't sure of your relationship as a child of God. If you have never made a public statement of your faith in Jesus Christ as your Savior and Redeemer. You will want to take time now to do the following steps because you will need the power of His Holy Spirit in you to become a follower of Jesus. Read Romans 3:21-26, which speaks of redemption through Christ and choose someone to whom you can make the following confession of faith—this can also be done as a group.

> *"But now the righteousness of God without the law is manifested, being witnessed by the law and the prophets; Even the righteousness of God which is by the faith of Jesus Christ unto all and upon all them that believe: for there is no difference: For all have sinned, and come short of the glory of God; Being justified freely by his grace through the redemption that is in Christ Jesus: Whom God hath set forth to be a propitiation through faith in his blood, to declare his righteousness for the remission of sins that are past, through the forbearance of God; To declare, I say, at this time his righteousness: that he might be just, and the justifier of him which believeth in Jesus."* —Romans 3:21-26

Prayer of Repentance & Confession of Faith

Lord, I repent of all the ways I have rebelled against Your love. I have chosen to be the lord of my own life and have tried to find joy and peace in all the wrong places. In search of peace and joy, I have violated Your will in many ways and brought grief to Your Holy Spirit. I do not want to walk in sin anymore. I need You, Jesus, to become the Lord of my life. Come, Lord Jesus, live in my heart and give me a new heart. Fill me with Your Holy Spirit that I may find my peace and joy in You and not in manmade "empty wells." In Jesus' name, Amen.

EQUIPPING FOR WARFARE

"Howbeit when he, the Spirit of truth, is come, he will guide you into all truth: for he shall not speak of himself; but whatsoever he shall hear, that shall he speak: and he will shew you things to come." —John 16:13

RECEIVING THE HOLY SPIRIT

The Holy Spirit is God

He is the third person of the Trinity. In the beginning, was God the Father, God the Son, and God the Holy Spirit. The Holy Spirit is God. The Holy Spirit is Omnipotent, He is all-powerful, almighty, and has unlimited power. He is omnipresent, meaning He is always everywhere. We can't escape from the presence of the Holy Spirit.

"In the beginning God created the heaven and the earth. And the earth was without form, and void; and darkness was upon the face of the deep. And the Spirit of God moved upon the face of the waters. And God said, Let there be light: and there was light.—"And God said, Let us make man in our image, after our likeness: and let them have dominion over the fish of the sea, and over the fowl of the air, and over the cattle, and over all the earth, and over every creeping thing that creepeth upon the earth." —Genesis 1:1-3, 26

The Holy Spirit is the Comforter

In John 16:7, Jesus told His disciples that He would soon leave them and ascend back to His Father, but He would not leave them alone. He promised He would send His Comforter to be with them—the Holy Spirit.

"Finally, brethren, farewell. Be perfect, be of good comfort, be of one mind, live in peace; and the God of love and peace shall be with you. Greet one another with an holy kiss. All the saints salute you. The grace of the Lord Jesus Christ, and the love of God, and the communion of the Holy Ghost, be with you all. Amen." —II Cor. 13:11-14

The Holy Spirit Knows the Thoughts of God

The spirit within each of us is 'the real us.' As we look at the Holy Spirit and hear His voice, what we are seeing, and hearing is the very heart of God.

"For what man knoweth the things of a man, save the spirit of man which is in him? even so the things of God knoweth no man, but the Spirit of God. Now we have received, not the spirit of the world, but the spirit which is of God; that we might know the things that are freely given to us of God." —I Corinthians 2:11-12

The Holy Spirit Glorifies Jesus

The Holy Spirit glorifies Christ by declaring Him or making Him known to us. It is the work of the Holy Spirit to throw light on Jesus Christ, Who is the image of the invisible God.

> *"He shall glorify me: for he shall receive of mine, and shall shew it unto you. All things that the Father hath are mine: therefore said I, that he shall take of mine, and shall shew it unto you."*—John 16:14-15

The Holy Spirit Convicts of Sin

The Holy Spirit is the one who will convict us of our sins and our need for Jesus. The Holy Spirit is our conscience. He does not bring condemnation, but He does bring conviction.

> *"And when he is come, he will reprove the world of sin, and of righteousness, and of judgment"* —John 16:8

The Holy Spirit Teaches and Reminds Us

It is the Holy Spirit who reveals to us the true meaning or intent of God's word. He reveals the heart of the Father to us through the written word of God.

> *"But the Comforter, which is the Holy Ghost, whom the Father will send in my name, he shall teach you all things, and bring all things to your remembrance, whatsoever I have said unto you."*—John 14:26

The Holy Spirit Will Speak Guidance to Us

It is the Holy Spirit Who will speak to and tell us the will of the Father. He is one with the Father and Jesus Christ.

> *"Howbeit when he, the Spirit of truth, is come, he will guide you into all truth: for he shall not speak of himself; but whatsoever he shall hear, that shall he speak: and he will shew you things to come."* —John 16:13

The Holy Spirit Helps Us to Pray

The Holy Spirit comes to "indwell" believers. He is the third person of the Trinity and abides in the hearts and souls of believers. When the Spirit of Truth comes, He will guide us into all Truth; for He shall not speak of Himself—He shall glorify God. He will show us God's heart for the person or situation for which we are praying. You may find yourself weeping, or in travail while praying. This is the Holy Spirit interceding through you on behalf of the person or situation God placed on your heart. Romans 8:26 states, *"Likewise the Spirit also helpeth our infirmities: for we know not what we should pray for as we ought: but the Spirit itself maketh intercession for us with groanings which cannot be uttered."*

The Holy Spirit Equips and Empowers Us with His Gifts

God never tells us to do something without giving us the ability to do it. He empowers us with His gifts. In I Corinthians 12, we find all the gifts of the Spirit that are available to those who receive the Holy Spirit. There are different kinds of service, but the same Lord. These are listed as wisdom, words of knowledge, faith, gifts of healing, miraculous powers, prophecy, discerning of spirits, speaking in tongues, and interpretation of tongues. The gifts are different from the offices spoken of in I Corinthians 12:27-30, where Paul explains that *"Now ye are the body of Christ, and members in particular. And God hath set some in the church, first apostles, secondarily prophets, thirdly teachers, after that miracles, then gifts of healings, helps, governments, diversities of tongues. Are all apostles? are all prophets? are all teachers? are all workers of miracles? Have all the gifts of healing? do all speak with tongues? do all interpret?"* Paul mentions the gifts of teaching, helps, and administration. In Romans 12:4-5, He emphasizes that we all have different gifts: *"For as we have many members in one body, and all members have not the same office: So we, being many, are one body in Christ, and every one members one of another."*

REFLECTIVE EXERCISE
Receiving the Holy Spirit

Identify the steps of personal spiritual preparation before entering the realm of inner healing and spiritual warfare. Recognize the ways God provided for the body of Christ to be empowered through the Holy Spirit to meet the needs of our brothers and sisters. Steps to receiving the Holy Spirit—For those who have been baptized but lack the power of the Holy Spirit; it may be that no one told you to look for the gifts or perhaps you have never had a teaching on the work of the Holy Spirit. Now is a good time to take the following steps to receive the full empowerment of the Holy Spirit of Jesus Christ.

KNOW GOD'S WORD

Without the Word of God, we can't face the trials and sufferings of life on this earth. As stated previously, the Word tells us in Ephesians 6:12, *"For we wrestle not against flesh and blood, but against principalities, against powers, against the rulers of the darkness of this world, against spiritual wickedness in high places."*

Hebrews 1:1-3—*"God, who at sundry times and in divers manners spake in time past unto the fathers by the prophets, Hath in these last days spoken unto us by his Son, whom he hath appointed heir of all things, by whom also he made the worlds; Who being the brightness of his glory, and the express image of his person, and upholding all things by the word of his power, when he had by himself purged our sins, sat down on the right hand of the Majesty on high;"*

Hebrews 4:12—*"For the word of God is quick, and powerful, and sharper than any two-edged sword, piercing even to the dividing asunder of soul and spirit, and of the joints and marrow, and is a discerner of the thoughts and intents of the heart."*

The Bible tells us, *"My people are destroyed for lack of knowledge…"*—Hosea 4:6a. The Word of God is to be our guide to a constructive, healthy, productive, successful life—a life that leads to righteousness and eternal life with God. It is a guide to keep us from destroying our lives.

WEAR THE ARMOR OF GOD

Consider what the Word says in Ephesians 6:11-18, *"Put on the whole armor of God, that ye may be able to stand against the wiles of the devil. For we wrestle not against flesh and blood, but against principalities, against powers, against the rulers of the darkness of this world, against spiritual wickedness in high places. Wherefore take unto you the whole armor of God, that ye may be able to withstand in the evil day, and having done all, to stand. Stand therefore, having your loins girt about with truth, and having on the breastplate of righteousness; And your feet shod with the preparation of the gospel of peace; Above all, taking the shield of faith, wherewith ye shall be able to quench all the fiery darts of the wicked. And take the helmet of salvation, and the sword of the Spirit, which is the word of God: Praying always with all prayer and supplication in the Spirit, and watching thereunto with all perseverance and supplication for all saints;"* —Ephesians 6:16-18

No Soldier Goes to Battle Without His Gear
No Christian Soldier Goes to Battle Without His Spiritual Armor

THE HELMET OF SALVATION

This piece of armor is designed to protect our minds and our attitudes towards those who are around us, at any given time. When the tempter comes to us with evil insinuations against the grace of God; we need this helmet of salvation to keep our head on straight.

The helmet of salvation ensures us the trustworthiness of God's promises; and His ability to save us to the utmost. We shouldn't rush into battle without the helmet of salvation firmly fixed upon our heads. Our salvation is secure, and our redemption is glorious.

Our minds are the playground of the enemy who loves to deceive and lie to us. When we believe these lies; he keeps us so focused on protecting ourselves that we shut out God and everyone who wants to help us. He will have us believing lies that will destroy our relationships as well as our positive self-images. As we meditate on God's word, it becomes written in our minds; causing us to become steadfast—having a guide (map) and rudder for our lives.

THE BREASTPLATE OF RIGHTEOUSNESS

It is with the breastplate of righteousness that we find clear and true protection. We ward off the attacks of the enemy when we understand that we are clothed with Christ's righteousness, and not our righteousness. As we walk in the ways of God; we are protected by God's promises. In Deuteronomy 5, Moses presents the *Ten Commandments* to God's people. The *Ten Commandments* were to be guidelines; showing them how to live their lives because God wanted His people to be prosperous, happy, and healthy.

> *"Ye shall walk in all the ways which the Lord your God hath commanded you, that ye may live, and that it may be well with you, and that ye may prolong your days in the land which ye shall possess.* —Deuteronomy 5:33

Additionally, Deuteronomy 6:24-25, states, *"And the LORD commanded us to do all these statutes, to fear the LORD our God, for our good always, that he might preserve us alive, as it is at this day. And it shall be our righteousness, if we observe to do all these commandments before the LORD our God, as he hath commanded us."*

We are to live as we have been called; doing right acts and right deeds in the sight of God. If we do this; our hearts won't condemn us, and the enemy can't condemn us. In other words, if our manner of life does not line up with our witness for Christ; we will be found without a breastplate; leaving us vulnerable to the enemy's attacks. Just as stated in Isaiah 59:17, *"For he put on righteousness as a breastplate, and an helmet of salvation upon his head; and he put on the garments of vengeance for clothing, and was clad with zeal as a cloak."* And is also stated in Romans 6:12-13, *"Let not sin therefore reign in your mortal body, that ye should obey it in the lusts thereof. Neither yield ye your members as instruments of unrighteousness unto sin: but yield yourselves unto God, as those that are alive from the dead, and your members as instruments of righteousness unto God."*

BELT OF TRUTH

Sometimes, we feel afraid of hurting the feelings of sensitive people when confronting them with the truth. We are also left with the feeling of having to walk on eggshells while confronting them. In other situations, we do not want to be honest with people whom we know are living in sin; they may get angry with us. Even though we see the price of how their sinful ways are negatively affecting them physically, mentally, and emotionally; we still lack the courage to tell them the truth. To avoid confrontation; we cushion the truth with half-truths, or color it with humor; allowing us to stay on good terms with them. By doing so, we aren't only giving them permission to be less than the person they can be; we are also enabling their behavior—enabling them to become deceivers. Thereby, when we hide the truth from them, we also enable ourselves to become deceivers. However, if we are going to be caregivers, we must walk in truth.

Ezekiel: 3:18-19 says, "When I say unto the wicked, Thou shalt surely die; and thou givest him not warning, nor speakest to warn the wicked from his wicked way, to save his life; the same wicked man shall die in his iniquity; but his blood will I require at thine hand. Yet if thou warn the wicked, and he turns not from his wickedness, nor from his wicked way, he shall die in his iniquity; but thou hast delivered thy soul."

THE SHOES OF PEACE

When we walk in line with God's Word by trusting Him, and trusting His Word to be true—we have peace. Children who live in a home where they know they are loved, and protected have peace. Knowing we are God's children who are saved by His grace, and protected by His covering causes us to live in peace. The lies of the enemy, when believed, rob us of our peace. If experiencing fear or anxiety, we aren't trusting in God's provision and protection.

A word found in Philippians 4:4-9 that has helped many people through tough situations can be divided into the following four steps:

1. *"Rejoice in the Lord always: and again I say, Rejoice. Let your moderation be known unto all men. The Lord is at hand."*
2. *"Be careful for nothing; but in everything by prayer and supplication with thanksgiving let your requests be made known unto God. And the peace of God, which passes all understanding, shall keep your hearts and minds through Christ Jesus."*
3. *"Finally, brethren, whatsoever things are true, whatsoever things are honest, whatsoever things are just, whatsoever things are pure, whatsoever things are lovely, whatsoever things are of good report; if there be any virtue, and if there be any praise, think on these things."*
4. *"Those things, which ye have both learned, and received, and heard, and seen in me, do: and the God of peace shall be with you."*

When following these steps—we will walk in the shoes of peace. We also rid ourselves of all manner of illnesses brought on by the body's reaction to disbelief, doubt, fear, and lack of faith in an almighty God, Who loves us. The shoes of peace increase our mobility; enabling us to move quickly and fearlessly over unfamiliar ground because we know our security is in Him.

THE SHIELD OF FAITH

Our faith is anchored in the person of Jesus Christ—Who He is, what He has done for us, and in nothing else; He is our shield. Habakkuk 2:4 states, *"Behold, his soul which is lifted up is not upright in him: but the just shall live by his faith."*

THE SWORD OF THE SPIRIT

The sword of the Spirit is the Word of God. Hebrews 4:12 states: *"For the word of God is quick, and powerful, and sharper than any two edged sword, piercing even to the dividing asunder of soul and spirit, and of the joints and marrow, and is a discerner of the thoughts and intents of the heart."* Jesus tells us in Matthew 10:34, *"Think not that I am come to send peace on earth: I came not to send peace, but a sword."*

Prayer for the Armor of God (Sample Prayer)

Dear Father,

I place upon myself the Helmet of Salvation. It serves as a reminder of my salvation and that I am a child of Yours, the King. I place upon myself the Breastplate of Righteousness, which covers my sins and weaknesses; protecting me from the attacks of the enemy that would condemn and deceive me. I place upon myself the Belt of Truth that keeps me steadfast in Your Word—it empowers me and enlightens my path to protect me. I place upon my feet the Shoes of Peace; provided by Your grace. I rejoice that You order my steps and go before me. You are Jehovah Shalom, my peace in times of trouble. I take up the Shield of Faith that protects me from the lies and deceptions of the enemy—protecting me from the fiery darts which are intended to wound me; hindering my walk with You, God. I take up the sword of the Spirit which is the Word of God, by speaking Your word with my mouth, to overcome the enemy with truth. Jesus' Name

Lesson Three

FAMILY TREE—GETTING TO THE ROOT

Lesson Three

Family Tree—Getting to the Root

""Either make the tree good, and his fruit good; or else make the tree corrupt, and his fruit corrupt: for the tree is known by his fruit." —Matthew 12:33

FAMILY ROOTS FEED THE TREE

Children thrive on love. Each life is a precious gift from God; created perfectly with His imprint on every spirit. Every life is planned by God for a purpose.

> *"For thou hast possessed my reins: thou hast covered me in my mother's womb. I will praise thee; for I am fearfully and wonderfully made: marvellous are thy works; and that my soul knoweth right well. My substance was not hid from thee, when I was made in secret, and curiously wrought in the lowest parts of the earth. Thine eyes did see my substance, yet being unperfect; and in thy book all my members were written, which in continuance were fashioned, when as yet there was none of them."* —Psalm 139:13-16

Each child's life is like a tapestry in the hands of God; weaving every circumstance of his life into the fabric and pattern He desires for each child. We grieve today, especially over the lives of our children whose spiritual well-being is sacrificed to the idols of this paganistic world. Most of the human service agencies are overloaded with cases of child abuse and neglect from parents who are on drugs or alcohol—who themselves were abused or neglected.

God instructed parents to impress His teachings upon their children, by talking about them at home. Parents were also instructed to model God's word for their children. As a Christian nation, our first schools were Christian schools where the focus was on teaching our children to read the Bible—the guidelines for living came from God's Word. Discipline was used to bring the child's will in line with God's will. Discipline was not to be used to punish or destroy, but to build character in the child. We all know that discipline can be abused when the parents themselves aren't under the authority of God. However, without proper guidance, children are like rudderless ships which are blown and tossed by the winds of the world. God's Word is like a rudder to guide them.

Many people who come for healing have been abused physically, sexually, emotionally, and psychologically. We are told in the third chapter of James about the power of the tongue which is used to either build up or to destroy. In this chapter, we will talk about the lies that mold and shape people's lives.

 *Reckless words pierce the heart like a sword, but the tongue of the wise brings healing.* —Proverbs 12:18

WORDS HAVE POWER

It is the words and actions written on the hearts of our children that guide them in their life's path. Some homes are fertile soil for healthy, wholesome children to grow and thrive. Other homes are like minefields where hidden bombs are ready to explode in their face; destroying their lives. Homes that provide acceptance, love, and security will usually produce healthy children—who know how to handle life's situations. Others who have to struggle to survive in a world filled with rejection, hatred, and depravity will be marred and given little with which to thrive. It is only by God's grace that some children survive. Of the survivors, many have numerous scars that take their lives down a twisted path that leads to disastrous results. Others, with God's help, rise above their circumstances and live lives that influence the world in very positive ways.

The book of Isaiah tells us about God's provision for the wounded.

> *"I, even I, am he that comforteth you: who art thou, that thou shouldest be afraid of a man that shall die, and of the son of man which shall be made as grass; And forgettest the LORD thy maker, that hath stretched forth the heavens, and laid the foundations of the earth; and hast feared continually every day because of the fury of the oppressor, as if he were ready to destroy? and where is the fury of the oppressor? The captive exile hasteneth that he may be loosed, and that he should not die in the pit, nor that his bread should fail. But I am the LORD thy God, that divided the sea, whose waves roared: The LORD of hosts is his name. And I have put my words in thy mouth, and I have covered thee in the shadow of mine hand, that I may plant the heavens, and lay the foundations of the earth, and say unto Zion, Thou art my people."* —Isaiah 51:12-16

We find that the roots of bondage are sown in early childhood—often in the womb. Studies have shown that the emotional, physical, and mental health of the mother while carrying the child in her womb can influence the child's development. When a mother does not want the child, the child senses the mother's emotional detachment and suffers rejection in the womb. Children who are adopted have an innate sense of losing the mother who carried them for nine months and has to re-bond with the new mother. The sense of separation from the birth mother is registered in the soul of the child. Detailed research shows the effects of the pregnant mother's mental, physical, psychological, and emotional well-being on their unborn child.

When a child has difficulty finding the safety, security, and acceptance necessary for normal and healthy development, seeds of frustration and anger are planted in his spirit. With sustained neglect of nurturing, this can develop into a focus on self. When these early needs go unmet, there is a constant gnawing away at the inner self. The child feels something is missing—a part of him is not like everyone else. The constant looking within to examine self, results in a constant self-evaluation and a perception that they aren't acceptable or lovable like other children. They experience jealousy and envy over others' obvious acceptance, deepening their anger and depression. These self-perceptions lead to the development of a sense of shame and guilt that they surround with walls of defenses to protect them from further emotional injury.

INCLUSION-CONTROL-AFFECT Diagram

ESTABLISHING BONDING AND HEALTHY RELATIONSHIPS

"Make a tree good and its fruit will be good, or make a tree bad and its fruit will be bad, for a tree recognized by its fruit." - Matthew 12:33

In order to bond with one another and to establish healthy relationships, children need to know they have the following components to family life::

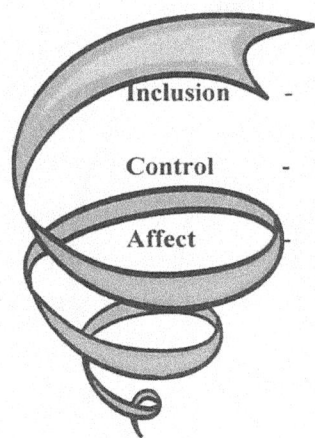

Inclusion — To know they are loved, safe, protected, secure, that someone cares for them

Control — Knowing they can master daily activities, and help themselves do what they see others doing.

Affect — To be able to affect change in the situation they find themselves, and know their ideas and thoughts are respected and contribute to making a difference.

Source, Proctor & Gamble Personal Growth and Development training event

REFLECTIVE EXERCISE

As you look back over the *INCLUSION-CONTROL-AFFECT Diagram*—note your thoughts, feelings, and beliefs about yourself and your family that you may want to ask God to shed His light on, for more understanding.

We, as believers in God, have a gauge to identify the lies we are being told—the Bible is our gauge. It is our plumb line, so to speak, that gives us a gauge with which to discern truth from a lie. God Himself is TRUTH, and His Word conveys truth. When His LIGHT is shed on our beliefs, it is like a two-edged sword.

Hebrews 4:12-13 says, *"For the word of God is quick, and powerful, and sharper than any twoedged sword, piercing even to the dividing asunder of soul and spirit, and of the joints and marrow, and is a discerner of the thoughts and intents of the heart. Neither is there any creature that is not manifest in his sight: but all things are naked and opened unto the eyes of him with whom we have to do."*

TREE OF BONDAGE vs. TREE OF FREEDOM *(Source unknown)*

"Either make the tree good, and his fruit good; or else make the tree corrupt, and his fruit corrupt: for the tree is known by his fruit." —Matthew 12:33

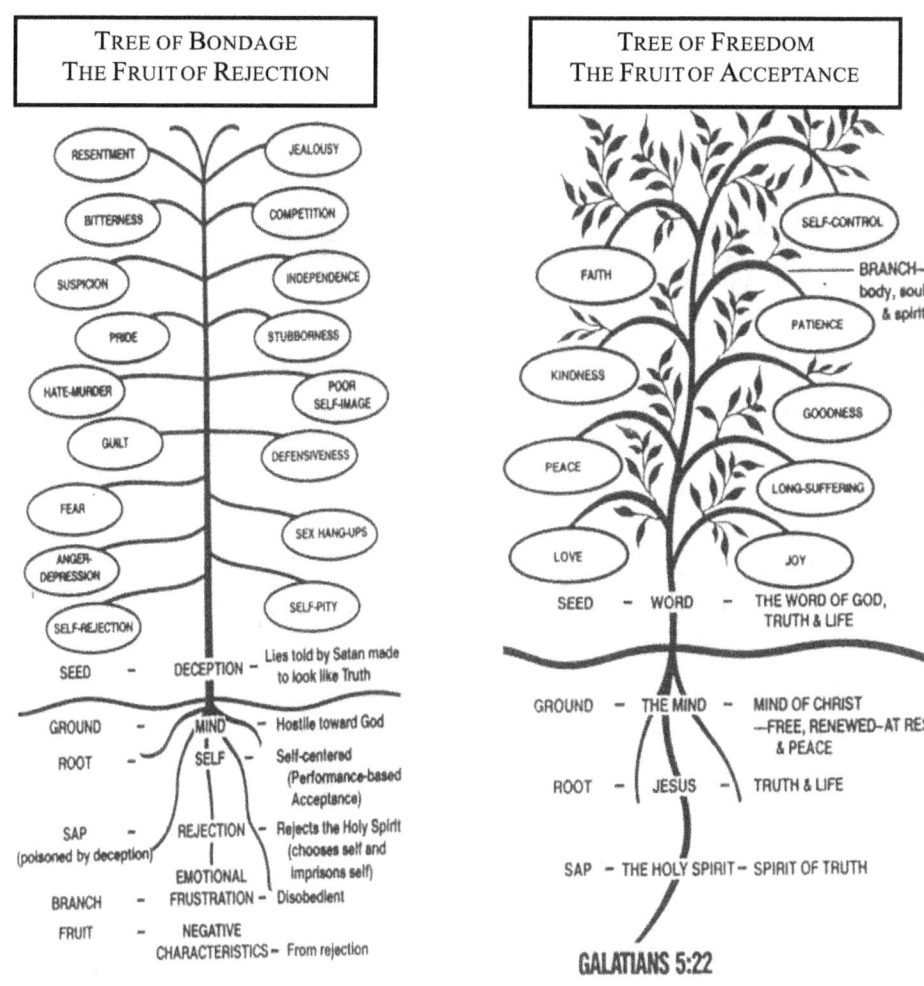

Lesson Four

FAMILY SYSTEMS— LAYING THE FOUNDATIONS

Lesson Four

Family Systems—Laying the Foundations

FAMILY SYSTEMS

The Family Systems Model demonstrates the influence the family has on forming the choices we make as individuals. It also demonstrates the impact of information gathered from our culture—schools, colleges, work, TV, Internet, newspaper and other media, books, church, and government. These all put pressure on the family system which either strengthens or weakens the system, and thereby affects the formation process.

The very formation of the family takes place at the point where two people come together in love to become one in marriage. Whether, it is conscious or unconscious both mates come together with hopes, dreams, values, roles, rules, and rituals in their hearts —hoping to create a family as good as or better than the family they grew up in. They will take from the best they know and try to re-create that—or knowing the worst, and try to do something different. In many cases, unwed couples who are seeking love and healing for their own lives give no thought to the development of a marriage or family. They come together trying to fulfill a need in their souls for what they didn't get from their families. We will look at an average couple; assuming they have in mind the ongoing growth of their love through marriage and a family. They bring with them a certain picture in their minds about the things they have learned in their lives that were meaningful to them. They will, whether consciously or unconsciously bring that about in their marriage and family.

God gave specific directions to families as to what would bring about the best scenario to provide health, happiness, and prosperity. We will look at several components that make up the healthy foundation of a family. As I look at the *Family Systems Chart*, (next page) I see an egg. We all know what an egg looks like. Those who have cooked with eggs recognize that each egg has a protective shell that contains the egg white and egg yolk. We recognize that some shells are harder than others; the membrane lining of the shell is stronger in some eggs than in others. I see the eggshell, representing the pledge or commitment of the man and woman while uniting as ONE body—taking on the responsibility of creating a family by patterning itself from the family structure as God intended. I see the membrane representing the beliefs, values, roles, rules, rituals, and standards which create the strength or weakness of the family unit.

THE FAMILY SYSTEMS MODEL

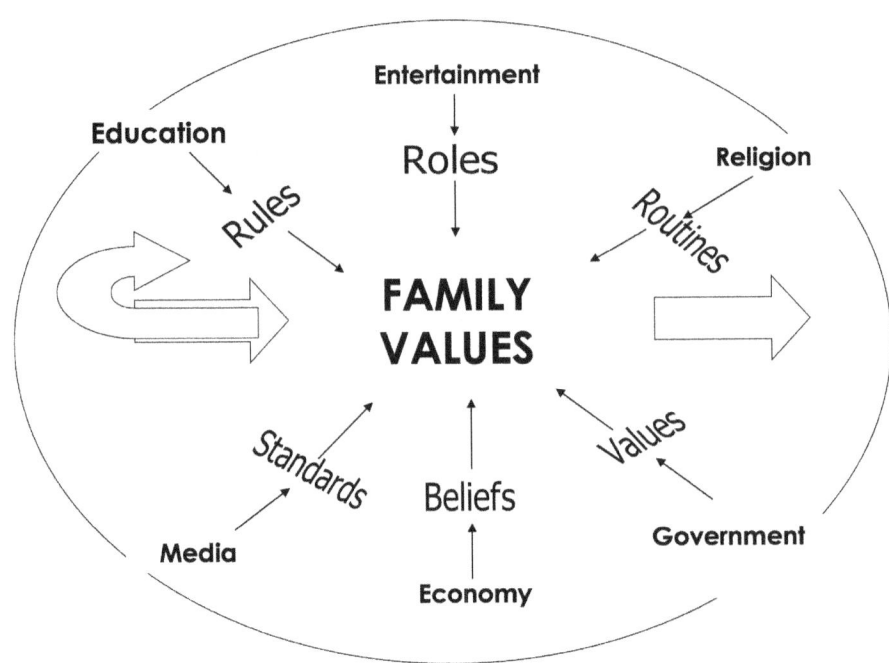

RULES

Parents are the child's first image of God. As we set things in order in our families, the child sees us as the person(s) who brings order, safety, and security. Parental discipline in modern times has come under heavy scrutiny by others, due to the misuse of correction and punishment. Discipline has also been unpopular, especially if the parents are divorced and the children must divide their time between two parents. Neither parent wants to be the disciplinary one; both parents are often trying to be friends with the child.

Children need consistency and order to know what is acceptable and not acceptable. Changing rules from place to place, from time to time is confusing to children. They need structure and stability—not necessarily a place where they can get by with anything. Discipline should always allow for restoration.

> *"But if any have caused grief, he hath not grieved me, but in part: that I may not overcharge you all. Sufficient to such a man is this punishment, which was inflicted of many. So that contrariwise ye ought rather to forgive him, and comfort him, lest perhaps such a one should be swallowed up with overmuch sorrow. Wherefore I beseech you that ye would confirm your love toward him. For to this end also did I write, that I might know the proof of you, whether ye be obedient in all things. To whom ye forgive any thing, I forgive also: for if I forgave any thing, to whom I forgave it, for your sakes forgave I it in the person of Christ; Lest Satan should get an advantage of us: for we are not ignorant of his devices."* —2 Corinthians 2:5-11

A child learns from instruction, but punishment brings shame and guilt which often leads to rebellion. Hebrews 12:10-12, offers us a bit of wisdom regarding discipline, *"For they verily for a few days chastened us after their pleasure; but he for our profit, that we might be partakers of his holiness. Now no chastening for the present seemeth to be joyous, but grievous: nevertheless, afterward it yieldeth the peaceable fruit of righteousness unto them which are exercised thereby. Wherefore lift up the hands which hang down, and the feeble knees;"*

A parent's role is not to judge and punish instead it is a role used to guide, teach, and direct. 2 Corinthians 2:5-11, teaches us the importance of not inflicting punishment on a person who has made a mistake, or who has done something wrong. These are times for teaching, not times for punishment. Paul urges us to reaffirm our love for the sinner. When this happens, the child will learn that he can move forward after a mistake. To punish and bring shame only causes a child to always be looking back at the pain; seeing himself as a bad person. This hinders a child's willingness to learn and move forward. The important lesson with mistakes is that we need to realize that we can grow wiser while learning from them. Remember, many great inventions have been created by making mistakes.

ROUTINES

According to Ecclesiastes 3:1-8, God ordained from the time of the creation—morning and night, light and dark, a time to lie down, a time to rise, a time to work, and a time to play. He designed man to work six days and rest the seventh day. Parents need to provide structure. He modeled a day for rest, worship, and times of celebration. God said that man would work from sunup until sundown, then rest. I heard a saying when I was a child that went like this; "Early to bed, early to rise, makes a man healthy, wealthy, and wise!" We all need structure. Children need structure to feel safe and secure. Children also need adequate sleep to grow. Parents need their time to spend together. Children must learn that parents have a life of their own and need time for their personal development—time to build and care for their relationship.

Repetition teaches good habits like brushing your teeth, combing your hair, and getting dressed to prepare for school, work, and church. It is a ritual that sets an example —on the seventh day, we go to church and worship. It is also a ritual that sets a precedent for celebrating an accomplishment, whether a job well done or a birthday. Celebration is part of life and marks significant occasions in our lives. That is why we as Christians celebrate Christmas, Easter, Pentecost, New Year's Day, Thanksgiving, etc. Each family needs special rituals like bedtime stories and having a family meal, giving the family opportunities to celebrate, bond, and communicate.

STANDARDS

The husband must manage his own family well and see that his children obey him with proper respect. *1 Timothy 3:4 says, "One that ruleth well his own house, having his children in subjection with all gravity;"* If anyone does not know how to manage his own family, how can he take care of God's church?

In Deuteronomy 5, God reveals His *Ten Commandments* for the direction and safety of His people—the Israelites. In Deuteronomy 6:6-9, He said to His people, *"And these words, which I command thee this day, shall be in thine heart: And thou shalt teach them diligently unto thy children, and shalt talk of them when thou sittest in thine house, and when thou walkest by the way, and when thou liest down, and when thou risest up. And thou shalt bind them for a sign upon thine hand, and they shall be as frontlets between thine eyes. And thou shalt write them upon the posts of thy house, and on thy gates."*

Do you set a standard for telling the truth even when a lie would get you what you want? Do you set a standard for doing a job to the best of your ability? Do you set a standard for cleanliness, punctuality, politeness, kindness, and settling conflicts peacefully? Without knowing it, our beliefs manifest in our behaviors and attitudes; causing us to act upon our beliefs. Our beliefs are either what "seems good in our own eyes" or gleaned from the Word of God—the Bible is the guide God provided for His people. In the New Testament, Jesus' words are filled with guidance regarding how to live our lives.

Hebrews 13:1-5 says, *"Let brotherly love continue. Be not forgetful to entertain strangers: for thereby some have entertained angels unawares. Remember them that are in bonds, as bound with them; and them which suffer adversity, as being yourselves also in the body. Marriage is honourable in all, and the bed undefiled: but whoremongers and adulterers God will judge. Let your conversation be without covetousness; and be content with such things as ye have: for he hath said, I will never leave thee, nor forsake thee.'"*

BELIEFS

Christianity is not just a set of beliefs. Christianity is a way of life, a community, and a way of life taught through the Bible and the Torah. Biblical teachings have become standards by which Christians judge right from wrong/good from evil. These guidelines or standards were established by God through His chosen prophets and apostles throughout the early years of mankind. We have seen the strength of the American family weaken due to the cultural changes that have removed God's principles from our schools, churches, businesses, media, entertainment, and government. Our educational system as well as every aspect of American life has been drastically altered by rebellion against God's Word. Parents, leaders, and teachers are expected to be advocators for these standards. The Apostle's Creed is one standard that is accepted by most of the Christian denominations. These basic beliefs are:

- There is one God, the Creator of the Universe.
- He created mankind in His image.
- God is omnipresent, omnipotent, and omniscient (present everywhere at one time, all-powerful, all-knowing).
- God is a person, Father to Jesus.
- Jesus is God's only Son who was conceived by the Holy Ghost, born of the Virgin Mary. He was crucified, dead, and buried. He descended to hell. On the third day, He rose again from the dead and ascended to heaven and sits at the right hand of God, the Father almighty, from whence He shall come to judge the living and the dead.
- Children are a gift from God.
- Every life has a divine purpose.
- The Holy Spirit unites us with God. When we accept Jesus as our Lord and Savior, His Holy Spirit comes to abide in our hearts.
- We are all part of the "family of God."
- Forgiveness of sins is one of the key marks of Christianity.
- Christ died to seal our forgiveness by God and thus have eternal life.
- The immortality of the soul and the resurrection of the body.

VALUES

Values are demonstrated in the way we live our lives and how we spend our time, money, and energy. Values are formed during three significant periods:

1. Imprint period from birth to 7 years of age
2. Modeling period from 8–14 years of age
3. Socialization period from 15–21 years

In Deuteronomy 5: 6-21, God laid down His written law for His chosen people whom He had delivered from slavery in Egypt. He recognized His people never had the freedom to rule themselves because they had been oppressed by wicked rulers. These laws were designed to make His chosen nation healthy, just, and merciful. When the people followed these laws, they prospered.

These personal values provide an internal reference for what is good, beneficial, important, useful, beautiful, desirable, constructive, etc. Values generate behavior and help solve common human problems. Our values in life will determine our goals and destiny.

Over time, the public expression of personal values that different groups find in their daily lives important is what lays the foundations of law, customs, and traditions. Personal values exist about cultural values and are either in agreement with or divergent from prevailing norms. A culture is a social system that shares a set of common values. These values permit social expectations and collective understandings of good beautiful, constructive, etc. Without normative personal values, there would be no cultural reference against which to measure the virtue of individual values, and cultural identity would disintegrate, divergent from prevailing norms.

Lesson Five
FAMILIES MAKE A DIFFERENCE

Lesson Five

Families Make a Difference

No two families are alike. While there are many combinations of family types, studies show that there are four different and clearly defined patterns of family life in our society. Look at the following family styles and see if you can identify yours.

THE FOUR BASIC TYPES OF FAMILIES

Source: Author unknown

1. AUTHORITARIAN

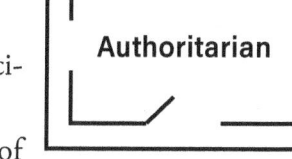

1. The authoritarian family is one in which the mother and father take responsibility for the safety and security of the family.
2. They assure that boundaries are in place to protect their children from accidents and injury.
3. They communicate love to each other and their children, assuring them of their importance to the family.
4. The lines of authority are identified and followed.
5. The rules are upheld by both parents so, children know they can't pit one parent against the other.
6. The family has routines which bind them together (e.g., eating meals together, going to church, stories at bedtime, vacations, Easter egg hunts, birthday and anniversary celebrations, etc.).
7. The home is where children are taught how to make choices and evaluate those choices and their consequences.
8. Mistakes are seen as opportunities to learn.
9. Each person is treated with respect.
10. Godly discipline and instruction are used—instead of condemnation and punishment when a child goes astray or uses poor judgment.

2. CHAOTIC

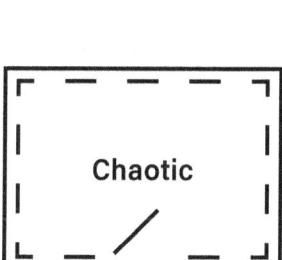

1. Neither parent is in charge.
2. Children are their parents.
3. Children "pit" one parent against the other.
4. There are no boundaries and no rules, discipline, or guidance.
5. Everyone does his own thing.
6. There are no meals together. Everyone fends for himself.
7. Children and parents come and go with little concern for the other.
8. House is "falling" around them: clutter, piles of dishes, and repairs left undone.
9. Children are often confused and desperate for parents to make decisions.
10. Children often take over parental roles.

3. RIGID

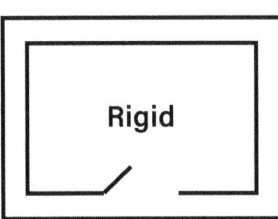

1. The rigid family is usually alienated from the world.
2. They keep to themselves and prefer not to be seen or known.
3. A parent is usually dictatorial and accountable to no one.
4. A parent rules with an "iron fist."
5. Rules are very rigid, frequently unbending, and subject to the parent's interpretation.
6. Harsh punishment is meted out for any who disobeys.
7. Those who are different are "outsiders."
8. What happens at home is "secret" and not revealed to "outsiders."
9. Punishment follows any "leaks."
10. Family "walks on eggshells" when Dad is home.
11. Family is manipulated by shame, guilt, demands, threats, lies, and abuse to keep them in line (including the spouse).
12. Family members feel weak and powerless.
13. Fear is the reigning force.

4. SHOWCASE

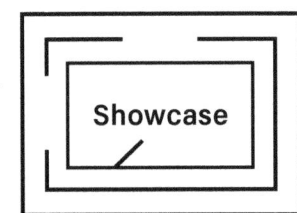

1. The showcase family will have all the appearances of a perfectly healthy family. But on the inside, there is much insecurity about who they are and how they are to act.
2. Often their rules, roles, beliefs, and values are inconsistent because the parents are unsure of who they are.
3. Often this is a family where parents have come from two different types of backgrounds; they know what they "should" be as a family, but lack the unity to make it happen.
4. Parents are insecure in their roles and vacillate between authoritative and rigid, or chaotic.
5. There is a lack of clear leadership.
6. Rules are Inconsistent.
7. Parents try to be friends with children rather than exercise parental authority.
8. Parents often are highly responsible and active in the church community.
9. Punishment vacillates between harsh and acquiescent.
10. Commitment is lacking to family rituals, traditions, vacations, and/or celebrations.
11. Family has difficulty dealing with conflict.
12. Communications are unclear.
13. There is a fear of anger and conflict.

BIBLICAL REFLECTION

I Timothy 5:8—*"But if any provide not for his own, and especially for those of his own house, he hath denied the faith, and is worse than an infidel."*

I John 5:18—*"We know that whosoever is born of God sinneth not, but he that is begotten of God keepeth himself, and that wicked one toucheth him not."*

Job 21:9—*"Their houses are safe from fear, neither is the rod of God upon them."*

I Peter 3:7—*""Likewise, ye husbands, dwell with them according to knowledge, giving honour unto the wife, as unto the weaker vessel, and as being heirs together of the grace of life; that your prayers be not hindered."*

REFLECTIVE EXERCISE

Identify the type of birth family you had (mother, father, and siblings) and describe how this family influenced your life. What has it taught you?

___

Describe your current family (you, your spouse, and children) and how this family has influenced your life. What has it taught you?

___

If you could write a motto for your birth family, what would it be? (e.g., Show the world we can take care of our own.)

___

BIBLICAL REFLECTION

Read these scriptures and take authority over the principalities of darkness that came upon you and your family. Jesus came to conquer Satan by His authority through the same Spirit He has given to us. When He died on the cross, He took our sins to the grave. He purchased our sins and the sins of our ancestors through His sacrificial blood. Afterward, He returned to heaven to live again.

> God has ordained through Christ that we would be given authority to trample on snakes and scorpions (the principalities of darkness). *"Behold, I give unto you power to tread on serpents and scorpions, and over all the power of the enemy: and nothing shall by any means hurt you."* —Luke 10:19

> *"According to the eternal purpose which he purposed in Christ Jesus our Lord: In whom we have boldness and access with confidence by the faith of him."* —Ephesians 3:11-12

> *"For this cause I bow my knees unto the Father of our Lord Jesus Christ, Of whom the whole family in heaven and earth is named, That he would grant you, according to the riches of his glory, to be strengthened with might by his Spirit in the inner man; That Christ may dwell in your hearts by faith; that ye, being rooted and grounded in love, May be able to comprehend with all saints what is the breadth, and length, and depth, and height; And to know the love of Christ, which passeth knowledge, that ye might be filled with all the fulness of God."* —Ephesians 3:14-19

PRAYER FOR BREAKING CURSES

Father God,
You made a way for me to be brought out of bondage through the blood of Jesus Christ, my Savior. Father, You are a jealous God—visiting the iniquity of the fathers upon the third and fourth generations of those who hate You; but showing mercy to those who love You and keep Your commandments. I am sorry for the sins of my ancestors. I am also sorry for their disobedience and rebellion against Your commandments. They broke Your heart and incurred Your judgment.

I, too, Lord, have the same sinful nature and have walked in ways that satisfied me at the sake of losing my relationship with You. Father, I need You, I need Your help, and Your guidance so I may not be led astray again. I need the help of Your Holy Spirit. Fill me, Lord, that I may be empowered to resist the temptations to return to the sins of my father. I take the sword of the Spirit that is Your Word and cut the spiritual bonds of sin between me, my family, and my ancestors. You have said that through our salvation, we are heirs to your Kingdom. I claim that inheritance for myself. In the name of Jesus Christ, our living Savior. Amen!

Lesson Six

GROWING UP IN STAGES

Lesson Six

Growing Up in Stages

We have all recognized people who seem to be stuck in their childhood behavior and thoughts. These are people who can't trust others, fear rejection, do not take chances, and are bound up in their fears or apprehensions. In addition, other debilitating behaviors include the inability to hold a job, keep relationships, verbally express opinions, and always must have the last word. We get impatient with adults acting like children. What prevents our ability to put our past behind us? It is easier "said" than done for some of us, yet the following scriptures indicate that we just need to, "put it behind us." Those of us who continue to have childlike behavior or childlike thinking need lots of unconditional love. We also need lots of help while working through our false beliefs and ineffective ways of trying to cope with problems.

"When I was a child, I spake as a child, I understood as a child, I thought as a child: but when I became a man, I put away childish things. For now we see through a glass, darkly; but then face to face: now I know in part; but then shall I know even as also I am known. And now abideth faith, hope, charity, these three; but the greatest of these is charity." —I Corinthians 13:11-13

In his book, *"Other Altars,"* Craig Lockwood explains in the chapter on Birth, Development, and Dissociation (pages 231–232); how trauma affects the developmental stages of a child and the effect of trauma on the brain.

- At birth, an infant's brain is filled with billions of neurons, the basic structural and functional unit of the nervous system, and is designed to recognize patterns in the world, so that stimuli, in the very beginning, start to be organized.
- In the first weeks, infants begin recognizing similar patterns and those that are different. They recognize interactions with their caregivers.

Next, infants begin to develop the "core self" which includes:
   a. The ability to do something themselves.
   b. Feeling connected to their bodies.
   c. Their emotional states.
   d. And/or history, that encompasses the other three categories.
   e. When trauma is experienced in childhood this "core" sense of self is profoundly injured.
   f. Thus, when children are abused their sense that they are the agents of their own will is damaged.
   g. Trauma, in other words, damages the "sense of agency," and when the victim's body is abusively intruded upon; trauma also damages the "sense of coherency." Through pain, the infant experiences feelings of rage and betrayal "Sense of affectivity". All this results in damage to the infant's "sense of continuity."

h. During the first twelve months, an infant's development is marked by very abrupt transitions between "states of alertness" and "states of mind." If there is no trauma in the relationship between the infant and its caregiver, the infant develops the ability during this period to transition to the next two development stages.

These two important "states" include the development of a "sense of self" and a "Sense of self with others," both of which are intertwined. A normal developed human being can't have a sense of who he is without having a sense of others.

Alan Shores, Professor at U.C.L.A., has conducted many studies on brain imagery. According to Professor Shores, the first eighteen months of a child's life is the most crucial time for bonding between him and his parents. In the first year, the child learns through his senses whether he is accepted or not; and whether or not he is a joy to his parents. He has identified two sensory tracks—left brain activity which interprets words and sounds, while the other track is the right brain which tracks voice tone and the look on the face. The child's brain will duplicate the exact emotion and register it in the neuron chemistry. According to Professor Shores' studies, three to nine months of age is the peak of bonding. He made a connection between the fact that many working mothers go back to work after the third month; thus, connecting to the growing numbers of children diagnosed with ADHD and ADD. The three-to-five-year age period is the next peak of bonding, and during this time the child is most apt to make an attachment to the father. The next big stage of bonding is between the ages of seven to ten with the age of fifteen being the last major step in bonding.

An infant who is traumatized by the caregiver never achieves the ability to smoothly make the transition between the development stages mentioned above. Parents who are impaired by alcoholism are rageful, physically or sexually abusive, or perhaps dissociate themselves and will change their behavior so quickly that the child will have a difficult time smoothing out his transitions because the parents can't alter theirs.

The following chart compares the development stages as reached by Erik Erikson and stages developed by Jean Illsley Clarke and Connie Dawson, authors of "*Growing Up Again*," Hazelden Education, 1989. Clarke and Dawson identify factors that contribute to developmental problems that require re-parenting. Their book is a course for working with people who had something happen to them that caused them to get "stuck" in a developmental stage that has kept them from maturing in that area.

Clarke and Dawson have identified clues that are indicators that adults need to experience by reparenting. Re-parenting is a technique that helps adults to identify what happened in their lives and in what developmental state it happened. To change the perceptions, beliefs, and behaviors surrounding that traumatic event, a painful adjustment or change must be made.

As we examine the chart, we will recognize the stages of growth and development of a normal child. There are minor differences between the two studies. However, we will study the clues that identify the age at the time of trauma.

Those of us who have had a difficult time trusting, have usually had a traumatic event occur during the first years of our lives. This is usually a very significant event. An excellent example of the significance of early childhood trauma is an adult in her mid-fifties who came for counseling. As we explored the root of this distrust and need to control, we realized that when she was born her twin sister died and her mother nearly died. She was sent to live with her grandmother while her mother recuperated in the hospital. The mother returned home but the child was left with the grandmother. Then the mother had another child and still the first child was not brought home. The grandmother insisted on the child being returned to the family only to have the child rejected, mocked, and mistreated. The child never found her place in the family. During her "growing up" years, she was treated as if she were invisible and was the brunt of everyone's jokes.

Learning to trust is one of the most significant lessons of life for a child because, if that trust is not developed, the child doesn't feel safe and secure in his environment. A child can only get his emotional, mental, physical, and spiritual needs met in a secure environment. Eventually, he will become mature enough to care for himself.

Child Development Chart by Erikson & Clarke

Source: Growing Up Again by Clarke and Connie Dawson, Hazeldon Educ.© 1992, Servant Publications

Erikson	Clarke/Dawson	Clues that indicate a need in the adult to grow up again.
1. Infancy (Trust vs. Mistrust) 0–1 year	**1. Being** 0–6 months	Not trusting others, wanting others to know your needs without your asking, not knowing what you need, not needing (feeling numb), believing others are more important, not trusting others to come through, not wanting touch or wanting it excessively or joyless sexual touching, unwilling to disclose self-information especially negative.
	2. Doing 6–18 months	Boredom, reluctance to initiate, overactive or over quiet, avoidance of doing unless perfect, compulsive neatness, not knowing what you know, believing it's okay not to be safe/protected/accepted
2. Early Childhood (Autonomy vs. Shame/doubt)	**3. Thinking** 18 mo–3 years	Inappropriate rebellion, rather be right than successful, bullying, use of anger to cover fear/sadness, thinking the world revolves around self, fear of anger in self or others, answering without thinking, so scared to say no and let others dominate, passive/aggressive.
3. Play Age (Industry vs. guilt)	**4. Identity and Power** 3–6 years	Having to be in a position of power, afraid of or reluctant to use power, unsure of personal adequacy, identity confusion or need to define self by a job or a relationship, driven to achieve, persistent outlandish dress or behavior, frequent comparison of self with others or needing to win, wanting or needing magical solutions of effects
4. School Age (Industry vs. Inferiority) 6–11 years	**5. Structure** 6–12 years	Having to belong to the gang, functioning well only as a loner, not understanding relevance of rules, not understanding freedom in rules, unwilling to examine self/values/morals, need to be King/Queen of the hill, trusting, thinking of group over self-thinking or intuition, expecting to have to do things without knowing/being taught how, reluctant to learn/be productive.
5. Adolescence (Identify vs. Identity Diffusion) 12–18 years	**6. Identity, Sexuality Separation** 13–19 years.	Preoccupation with sex, body, appearance, friends, sex role, vulnerable to peer pressure, unsure of own values, problems starting/ending jobs/roles/relationships, over-dependence on or alienation from family and others, irresponsibility, unable to make/keep commitments/looks for definition of self in others, confusion of nurturing and sex, unsure of sexual identity or lovable-ness.
6. Young Adulthood (Intimacy vs. Isolation) **7. Adulthood** (Generatively vs. Stagnation/Self-Absorption) **8. Senescence** (Integrity vs. Disgust/despair)	**7. Interdependence / Adulthood**	Leave home but return several times, unable to become separate/capable, decisive and supportive adults, break all the rules so that parents must force them to leave, never leave home/parents, leave but remain over dependent out of fear or lack of initiative, independent to the exclusion of interdependence, role inflexibility, fear of growing old, difficulty saying hello/good bye, unwilling to grieve and move on, living in past/future, living through others, not knowing/not getting what is needed, denial and discounting, codependency.

BIBLICAL REFLECTIONS

I John 4:4—*"Ye are of God, little children, and have overcome them: because greater is he that is in you, than he that is in the world."*

Psalm 127:3—*"Lo, children are an heritage of the LORD: and the fruit of the womb is his reward."*

Mark 10:14-16—*"But when Jesus saw it, he was much displeased, and said unto them, Suffer the little children to come unto me, and forbid them not: for of such is the kingdom of God. Verily I say unto you, Whosoever shall not receive the kingdom of God as a little child, he shall not enter therein. And he took them up in his arms, put his hands upon them, and blessed them."*

REFLECTIVE EXERCISE
Reflection on Trust vs. Distrust

What are your experiences with distrust? (Where? When? How? What? Who?)

___

Identify your feelings when you sense you can't trust a person or situation.

___

Identify your thoughts connected to your feelings.

___

REFLECTIVE EXERCISE
Developmental Scars

Look at the developmental charts and identify something that happened to disrupt your development growth. Identify clues to learn how and when a crisis affected your development growth. (Clues—insecurity, inability to trust, bonding issues, temper tantrums, rage, wanting power, sexual issues, aggressive behavior, etc.)

___

As we discussed the Tree of Life vs. Bondage—What did you identify about your own roots? And what type of "fruit" is on your tree?

___

While observing the Child Development Chart by *Erikson & Clarke*—Identify your most difficult time in life? What happened to you during that time? And how did it affect you?

___

What perception of life came from these events?

___

What lies have you believed?

___

What oaths or inner vows did you make as a result of the lies?

___

Why it is hard for some people to put their past behind them?

___

PRAY and ask the Lord to reveal any lies that still linger to hinder your healing.
ASK Jesus to show His truth regarding this event.
PRAY for forgiveness for those who lied to you or hurt you.
PRAY to break all oaths or inner vows you made as a child that are still guiding your life.

PRAYER FOR THE HEALING OF DEVELOPMENTAL SCARS

Father God,
You are my Creator, and You are omnipotent; which means You know everything. I give you permission to reveal to me any events that caused fear, terror, or trauma in my life that would have caused me to _____. (Pause to allow the Lord to reveal hurtful, painful events. Do not run or hide from the truth—make note of the event[s]).

_____
_____
_____

Father, amid this pain, I believed a lie that has resulted in much anguish in my life. Please reveal to me the lie(s) I have believed about myself, others, and You. (Allow yourself to be still while God reveals the lies you believed. Make note of the lie(s).

_____
_____
_____

Now, Father, I repent of embracing this (these) lie (s), because it has shaped my life in ways neither You, nor I ever planned on happening. I choose now, as an adult, to renounce this/these lie(s) and replace it with Your truth. Father, please speak Your truth to me so that I may be set free from the bondage of this/these lie(s). Make note of the truth God reveals to you.

_____
_____
_____

Father, thank You for Your truth that has set me free. I praise You for loving me and for being with me. Forgive me for my unbelief. Grant me forgiveness as well as Your grace to receive Your word as truth; and the joy to walk in Your truth. In Jesus' name, I ask. Amen.

Lesson Seven

TAKING THE AX TO THE ROOT

Lesson Seven

Taking the Ax to the Root

"For I, the Lord your God am a jealous God, punishing the children for the sins of their fathers to the third and fourth generation of those who hate me, but showing love to a thousand generations of those who love me and keep my commandments." —Deuteronomy 5:9b-10

GENERATIONAL SINS

Genealogies have become very popular since the decade of the 1960s. Websites, books, and other resources have been made available to us. These resources are readily accessible so we may discover who our ancestors are and learn something about the history of their life. Often, we see generational traits and characteristics passed down through many generations. In this study, we are interested in the spiritual heritage of our ancestors.

When Moses brought the Israelites out of Egypt, God had a plan to bless them. They had been in captivity for four hundred thirty years serving as slaves in Egypt. Owning nothing and having no "say" in what happened to them, the Israelites were subservient to the Egyptians. Being powerless, they developed a very dependent nature, always looking for others to care for their needs. The Israelites were exhilarated as God through Moses was setting them free from captivity. Moses led them into the desert away from their oppressive captors and began to re-civilize them.

No other people saw God work in such a powerful way. God spoke to the Israelites out of the fire by night, and the cloud by day. He took one nation out of another by demonstrating His mighty hand through miraculous signs and wonders before their very eyes. The Lord displayed these acts before the Israelites, hoping they might understand, He was God. He also opened their ears to hear His voice from heaven. He did this because He wanted to discipline them—He loved their forefathers and chose them as His people.

The Lord drove out evil nations before them to bring His people into the land of their inheritance. His last act before sending them into the Promised Land was to give them standards for self-rule. God knew that the Israelites would need guidelines for their lives. Knowing that Moses would not be going with them into the Promised Land, God gave Moses the *Ten Commandments* as their guidelines for living. Obedience to these commandments would ensure that all would go well with them and their children in the land He was giving them. The Israelites would need to look to God for direction since Moses would not be with them. These *Ten Commandments* are just as important guidelines today, as they were to the Israelites when Moses led them through the wilderness centuries ago.

TEN COMMANDMENTS
Deuteronomy 5:6-21, Exodus 20:1-17

1. *"I am the LORD thy God, which brought thee out of the land of Egypt, from the house of bondage. Thou shalt have none other gods before me."*
2. *"Thou shalt not make thee any graven image, or any likeness of anything that is in heaven above, or that is in the earth beneath, or that is in the waters beneath the earth: Thou shalt not bow down thyself unto them, nor serve them: for I the LORD thy God am a jealous God, visiting the iniquity of the fathers upon the children unto the third and fourth generation of them that hate me, And shewing mercy unto thousands of them that love me and keep my commandments."*
3. *"Thou shalt not take the name of the LORD thy God in vain: for the LORD will not hold him guiltless that taketh his name in vain.*
4. *"Keep the sabbath day to sanctify it, as the LORD thy God hath commanded thee. Six days thou shalt labour, and do all thy work: But the seventh day is the sabbath of the LORD thy God: in it thou shalt not do any work, thou, nor thy son, nor thy daughter, nor thy manservant, nor thy maidservant, nor thine ox, nor thine ass, nor any of thy cattle, nor thy stranger that is within thy gates; that thy manservant and thy maidservant may rest as well as thou. And remember that thou wast a servant in the land of Egypt, and that the LORD thy God brought thee out thence through a mighty hand and by a stretched out arm: therefore the LORD thy God commanded thee to keep the sabbath day.*
5. *"Honour thy father and thy mother, as the LORD thy God hath commanded thee; that thy days may be prolonged, and that it may go well with thee, in the land which the LORD thy God giveth thee.*
6. *"Thou shalt not kill."*
7. *"Neither shalt thou commit adultery."*
8. *"Neither shalt thou steal."*
9. *"Neither shalt thou bear false witness against thy neighbour."*
10. *"Neither shalt thou desire thy neighbour's wife, neither shalt thou covet thy neighbour's house, his field, or his manservant, or his maidservant, his ox, or his ass, or any thing that is thy neighbour's."*

BLESSINGS AND CURSES

For every infraction of the law of God, there are consequences to pay. Our obedience to these laws given by God will bring blessings, but disobedience will bring curses. The Bible tells us in Deuteronomy 28, the types of blessings we will receive if we are obedient to His laws, and the various curses that will be encountered when we are disobedient.

BLESSINGS—Obedience
—Deuteronomy 28:1-15
Protection   Prosperity
Exaltation   Victory
Health   God's Favor
Long Life   Reproduction

CURSES—Disobedience
—Deuteronomy 28:15-68
Humiliation   Failure
Barrenness   God's Disfavor
Unfruitfulness   Mental/ Physical
Poverty   Family Breakdown
Defeat   Oppression

As we examine our family history, we usually look for things that are significant about leadership roles in the community, wealth, occupations, nationalities, etc. Yet, the most important characteristic that gets passed down from generation to generation is the character of the person, and how they relate to the world around them. Those who walk in God's ways are usually benevolent in giving of their wealth as well as giving of themselves. They will characterize the life of Christ and blessings will flow from their lineage. Others who choose to live in rebellion to God's laws for whatever reason, will manifest broken lives and broken relationships. However, just as great men and women in the Bible sinned; due to their humble repentance and God's grace, God was able to use them in mighty ways.

God has a mighty plan for every person's life, even though we may mark our lives with sin. God is gracious and does not want to lose a single one from His family. As we examine our genealogies and families in the light of God's Word—use the tools of prayer and intercession. God can set us free from these bondages to our sins and the sins of our ancestors. Hallelujah!

According to God's Word, we read, *"But when the Pharisees had heard that he had put the Sadducees to silence, they were gathered together. Then one of them, which was a lawyer, asked him a question, tempting him, and saying, Master, which is the great commandment in the law? Jesus said unto him, Thou shalt love the Lord thy God with all thy heart, and with all thy soul, and with all thy mind. This is the first and great commandment. And the second is like unto it, Thou shalt love thy neighbour as thyself. On these two commandments hang all the law and the prophets."* —Matthew 22:34-40

REFLECTIVE EXERCISE
Blessings and Curses

Read the passages from Deuteronomy 28:1-68, to learn about generational traits and characteristics that get passed down through generations. In this section, we are interested in the "spiritual heritage" of our ancestors. God gives us His plan for mankind and also gives us a "blueprint" in the *Ten Commandments* for peace and prosperity. God promises to bless and prosper us if we follow His commands. But we also recognize that if we choose not to follow His directions, we will suffer consequences in our lives.

Write what you perceive to be generational blessings and curses in your life.

_____
_____
_____

Give your thoughts about the blessings and curses principle at work in your family? In your community? In our nation?

_____
_____
_____

PRAYER FOR BREAKING GENERATIONAL CURSES

Father God,

You made a way for me to be brought out of bondage through the blood of Jesus Christ, my Savior. Father, you are a jealous God, visiting the iniquity of the fathers upon the third and fourth generations of those who hate You, but showing mercy to those who love You and keep Your commandments. I am sorry for the sins of my ancestors and for their disobedience and rebellion against Your commandments. They broke Your heart and incurred Your judgment.

I, too, Lord, have the same sinful nature and have walked in ways that satisfied me at the sake of losing my relationship with You. Father, I need You, I need Your help, guidance, and direction so that I may not be led astray again. I also need the help of Your Holy Spirit.

Fill me, Lord, that I may be empowered to resist the temptations of returning to the sins of my forefathers. I take the sword of the Spirit which is Your Word and cut the spiritual bonds of sin between me, my family, and my ancestors. You have said that through our salvation we are heirs to your Kingdom. I claim that inheritance for myself and my family. In the name of Jesus Christ, our living Savior. Amen

ROOTS OF BITTERNESS

Sin affects us spiritually, emotionally, physically, and relationally. We all have a basic need to survive. Though Elijah had destroyed all the evil prophets with his sword, when his life was threatened by Jezebel; he was afraid and ran for his life. (See I Kings 19:1-14) He had enough of her intimidations and prayed that he might die. However, Elijah felt no less the victor than his ancestors; he fell asleep quite disgusted with himself. Even in victory, he was bitter and self-condemning. In his own eyes, Elijah saw himself as a grasshopper compared to Jezebel's forces.

In the story of the prodigal son, the older son reveals his bitterness towards everyone for rewarding his prodigal brother with a party. Attention was lavished on the prodigal son, even though he took the divided portion of his inheritance—ran, and squandered it. The older son was resentful that he had not been rewarded for all his years of faithful service. Bitterness blocked his ability to rejoice over his younger brother who was lost but now found. The prodigal was the son who realized the error of his ways and humbly repented for his sin.

How rarely do we find *goodwill* around us today? Angry drivers scream at each other in the streets. People fight to be first in line. Disgruntled employers and employees both demand their rights, but the common bond of God's people should be *goodwill*. Those with *goodwill* think the best of others, assuming that others have good motives, and intend to do what is right. When someone crosses us and we feel our "blood boil," How do we respond? We need to stop and ask ourselves, "How can I show this person *goodwill?*"

BIBLICAL REFLECTIONS

Study these scriptures and make notes on each cause of bitterness.

Matthew 27: 3, Genesis 4:1-8, Exodus 17:1-3, Numbers 20:7-12

1. Identify how bitter roots affect a person's ability to make wise decisions.
_____
_____
_____

2. Identify ways in which you find yourself reacting to bitter roots.
_____
_____
_____

Proverbs 14:10
"The heart knoweth his own bitterness; and a stranger doth not intermeddle with his joy."

Acts 8:23
"For I perceive that thou art in the gall of bitterness, and in the bond of iniquity."

THE GENOGRAM

The Genogram is an instrument developed through family systems research. It was designed to help us form a picture or profile of our family—to help assess the type of family system we grew up in, and to understand the inter-dynamics that make us who we are today. Studies have shown that the family has the greatest impact on our lives regarding how we see ourselves and our world.

"Hear, O Israel: The LORD our God is one LORD: And thou shalt love the LORD thy God with all thine heart, and with all thy soul, and with all thy might. And these words, which I command thee this day, shall be in thine heart: And thou shalt teach them diligently unto thy children, and shalt talk of them when thou sittest in thine house, and when thou walkest by the way, and when thou liest down, and when thou risest up. And thou shalt bind them for a sign upon thine hand, and they shall be as frontlets between thine eyes. And thou shalt write them upon the posts of thy house, and on thy gates." —Deuteronomy 6:4-9

In Proverbs, we are told, *"Train up a child in the way he should go: and when he is old, he will not depart from it."* —Proverbs 22:6

In Deuteronomy, God says, *"…for I the LORD thy God am a jealous God, visiting the iniquity of the fathers upon the children unto the third and fourth generation of them that hate me, And shewing mercy unto thousands of them that love me and keep my commandments."* —Deuteronomy 5:9a-10

"Even so we, when we were children, were in bondage under the elements of the world: But when the fulness of the time has come, God sent forth his Son, made of a woman, made under the law, To redeem them that were under the law, that we might receive the adoption of sons. And because ye are sons, God hath sent forth the Spirit of his Son into your hearts, crying, Abba, Father. Wherefore thou art no more a servant, but a son; and if a son, then an heir of God through Christ." —Galatians 4:3-7

Even though this is written for us and is a promise to us if we do not have this revelation, we can't claim this promise for ourselves and our families—the old oaths and vows of our ancestors will still apply to our lives today.

HOW TO USE THE GENOGRAM

The *Genogram* is a way to identify those things in life that have impacted our families. The family, through its attitudes, beliefs, and ways of responding to life plus, the ways those things are modeled for us—set the examples for how we are to live our lives. As children, we may not question the core values of our family, but we do learn from those around us.

Looking more closely at our families—a helpful tool may be used to assist with this important and valuable exercise. *The Personal Inventory Questionnaire* (found in the back of the book), is a useful tool used to probe into our past and to examine our current life status in multiple areas. Many people have forgotten some of the details of their growing-up years—the questionnaire asks probing questions to help you remember things you may have forgotten over time. This tool is also quite useful for anyone in the *helping profession* who has been or could be helpful to you in this journey. It provides an overall picture of who you are and where you have come from in a relatively short amount of time.

This questionnaire is also useful in uncovering one's spiritual past. It can pinpoint activities done knowingly or unknowingly, willingly or unwillingly; so, they may be cleansed from the ungodly spirit. As we learn of their potential for harm, we learn how to cleanse the harmful seeds planted perhaps many years ago. As our spirit becomes cleansed, healing can come. So, their spirit may be cleansed.

Using this tool, we can begin the process of filling in our *Genogram*—a tool used to identify patterns (positive and/or negative) that may have been passed down from generation to generation. As we examine our families, we will want to focus on the following:

- Spiritual strongholds of the enemy in the family history (e.g., rebellion, lying, unfaithfulness, abuse, etc.
- Family beliefs, rituals, roles, rules, and values
- Sins passed down from generation to generation (e.g., alcoholism, sexual abuse, divorce, adultery)
- Patterns of interaction within the family (e.g., men and women are segregated, strong dominating women and weak men, or strong dominating men and weak women; boys cherished, while girls are ignored; children can be seen but not heard)
- Roots of bitterness hatred, revenge, stubbornness, unforgiveness

HOMEWORK

- Identify your family portrait by completing the three-generation family *Genogram* on a separate piece of paper.
- Taking what you have learned through these first four lessons, identify the fruit that has grown on your family tree.

- Identify the roots of good and evil and the fruit caused by both good and evil roots (principalities). Pray for your family.

Your instructor will help you complete your *Genogram,* and will also help you identify the features that shaped your family profile. Remember, the changes that took place in our culture from Lesson One, *CHANGING TIMES, and* identify the elements of change in today's culture that affected your family profile. You can also use a larger sheet of paper. HINT: If you don't remember details, ask family members, older siblings, aunts, and uncles. Old Pictures/videos are also a great source of remembrance.

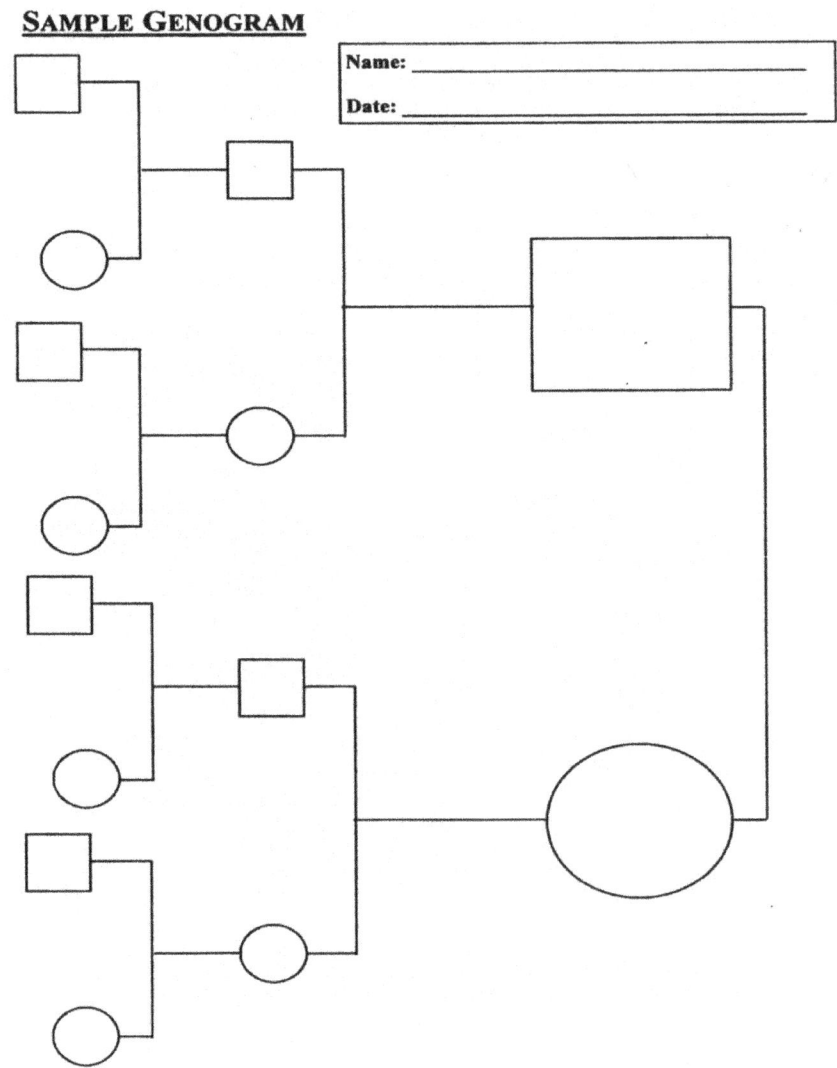

LOOKING FOR ROOT CAUSES OF PROBLEMS

As we try to help others whose backgrounds aren't known, it helps to look first at their family history. It is easier for them to talk about other family members rather than themselves, and also gives them time to develop a trusting relationship with the helper. It also gives us as "helpers" an understanding of where that person has walked and can help us in establishing compassion and empathy for this seeker's journey.

To get to the root of the problems, it will be helpful to look at family dynamics surrounding the following types of problems:

- Birth and birth order
- Untimely or timely deaths, unusual cases (stillbirth, accident, suicide)
- Miscarriages, abortions, stillbirths, births out of wedlock
- Marriages/divorces
- Occupation of both parents and those of generations past
- Ethnic background and cultural heritage
- Socio-economic level
- Religious affiliation
- Education
- Roles (male/female, strengths/weaknesses)
- Values and belief systems
- Mottos (one message you always heard from your family)
- Relationship of family members (close, distant, cohesive, divisive)
- How love was expressed
- How anger was expressed
- How critical incidents were handled
- Communications regarding—money, sex, children, alcohol/drugs, death, and religion
- Parenting Style (Strict, passive, neutral)
- Lifestyle

REFLECTIVE EXERCISE

Reflect on three generations of your family, beginning with yourself. Describe the personality and characteristics as well as significant things you remember about your siblings, parents, and grandparents. It is just as significant to describe a person whether he has been absent or present in some way from the family. All these things must be noted (e.g. prison, mental hospital, divorced, etc.)

Identify the significant characteristics that you see in your dad's family and those things that characterize your mother's family.

- What roles did men/women/children play in your family?
- What problems seemed to "plague" your family?
- What were your family beliefs/values/mottos?
- Identify the patterns of interaction within the family (i.e., cohesive, conflicting, chaotic, democratic, etc.)
- Identify any roots of bitterness and how they seem to manifest themselves.
- What are the spiritual strongholds of the enemy in your family as a result of your family interactions (i.e., unforgiveness, anxiousness, vengefulness, alienation, etc.)?

- How do you see professions or jobs being repeated throughout your family history?
- What influence did your parents' heritage have on your life?
- How did your family's religious affiliation affect you and how do you see yourself?
- How did your family's educational level influence your social or economic development?
- How was love expressed in your family? (men/women)
- How was anger expressed in your family? (men/women)
- Identify emotional defenses and toxic issues surrounding the following issues: Money, Sex, Parenting, Children, Alcohol Abuse

HOW TO USE THE INFORMATION THAT YOU FIND

Below is a sample of a completed *Genogram*—note the symbols you can use to describe life circumstances experienced by members of your family e.g., abortion, stillbirth, suicide, twins, death, divorce, separation, etc. You can use these symbols, and those you create to help you note the specific types of situations your family experienced.

Now that we have more information about our families, we will want to examine the impact of these things on our ensuing generations. Similar to looking for clues to a crime, you will use your discernment to look for patterns that seem to flow through the family. The information will be used to help us in the following biblical steps of the healing process:

- To guide us in severing unhealthy or sinful bonds from the past, even from the womb, that are affecting us today —Ezekiel 18:19-29
- To examine and change faulty beliefs —II Corinthians 10:3-5
- To identify unhealthy patterns of family interaction and replace them with ones prescribed by God's Word —I Corinthians 13:11
- To bring repentance and forgiveness —Acts 8:23
- To facilitate the process of dying to the old self and living in Christ —Ephesians 4:14-15
  To shed the light of God's Word into the darkness —I Corinthians 4:5

EXAMPLE OF A COMPLETED GENOGRAM

The following Genogram is often used as a real-life example of a completed Genogram. As we examine this Genogram of Alexander Graham Bell's family, we notice the progression of certain characteristics and other things passed down through the generations.

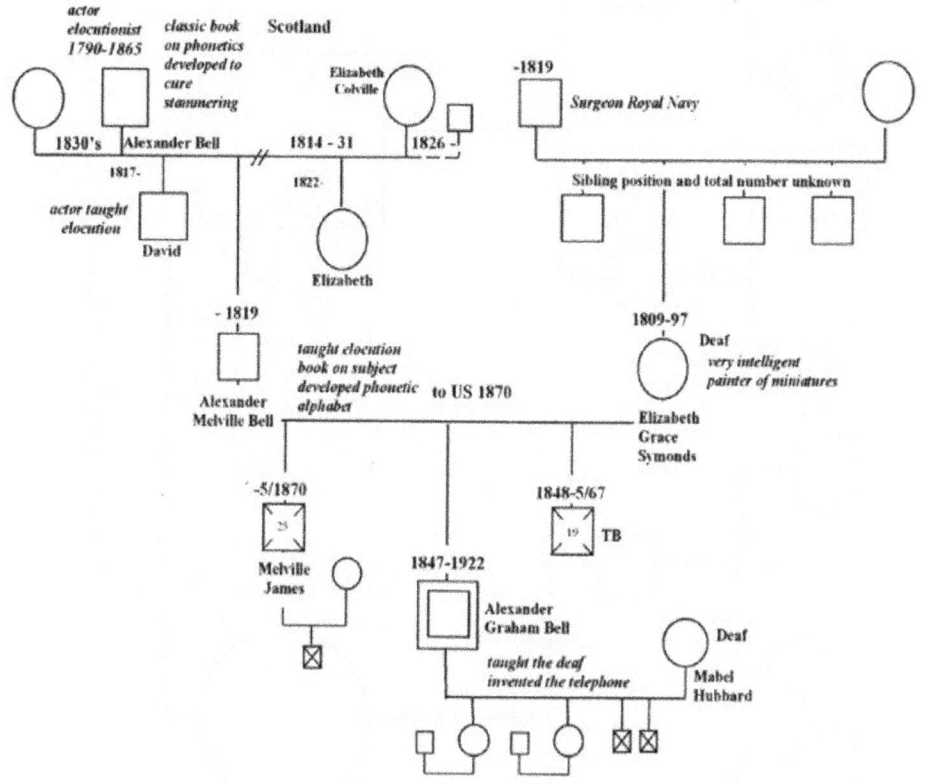

The diagram above provided courtesy of GENOGRAMS in Family Assessment by Monica McGoldrick and Randy Gerson., © 1985

GENOGRAM SYMBOLS

Diagram 2.1 Gender Symbols

Male ☐   Female ○

Diagram 2.2 Index person symbols

Male I. P. ☐   Female I.P. ◉

Diagram 2.3 Birthdates and Deathdates

Birthdate → 43-62 ← Deathdate

Diagram 2.4 Symbols for pregnancy, miscarriage, abortion, and stillbirth

pregnancy △   stillbirth ⊠ or ⊗   spontaneous abortion ●   induced abortion ✕

Diagram 2.5 Marriage Connections

M. 48

Diagram 2.6 Separations and divorces

M.22 S.28 D.40

Diagram 2.7 A husband with several wives

M.55 D.59   M.60 D.70   M.80 S.83

Lesson Eight

WALLS WE BUILD

Lesson Eight

Walls We Build

"And the fortress of the high fort of thy walls shall he bring down, lay low, and bring to the ground, even to the dust." —Isaiah 25:12

"There is a way which seemeth right unto a man, but the end thereof are the ways of death." —Proverbs 14:12

As human beings, we are tremendously resilient and creative in our methods of protecting ourselves—it is the drive we have for survival. Adam and Eve exercised their prerogative, they chose to defend themselves rather than confess their sin to God.

> *"And when the woman saw that the tree was good for food and that it was pleasant to the eyes, and a tree to be desired to make one wise, she took of the fruit thereof, and did eat, and gave also unto her husband with her; and he did eat. And the eyes of them both were opened, and they knew that they were naked; and they sewed fig leaves together, and made themselves aprons."* —Genesis 3:6-7

FIG LEAVES AND ALIBIS

Adam and Eve knew they had been disobedient because shame and guilt came upon them. They knew what God said, but the serpent twisted the truth. He lied about God's reason for telling them not to eat the fruit. As they began to question God, the serpent then lied by telling them that they didn't have to obey God because God wanted to keep all the power and pleasure for Himself. They immediately covered their sin by sewing fig leaves onto themselves. The fig leaves represent the lies we tell to defend ourselves. Adam and Eve stood before God telling lies, putting the blame on each other, and on the serpent. By covering themselves, they were trying to hide their sin from God—Who knows everything. God wants us to stand naked before Him in honesty and transparency. Adam and Eve chose to disobey God and they suffered the consequences of their sin.

God does not mix His words of punishment with the honey of grace—He is quick to punish evil. The American people in many ways have turned their faces from acknowledging sin by denying the acknowledgment of their sinful ways. Many want to pacify people who feel guilt and shame by *sewing fig leaves* onto them—telling them they do not need to be ashamed or feel guilty because they are just human; everyone sins. This discounts our need to confess and repent, a very basic principle of healing. In the 1960s, 'Situation Ethics' by Joseph Fletcher, taught that sin is irrelevant, which laid the groundwork for whitewashing the Word of God. "Situation Ethics" would have us believe that God uses different measures for different people. However, we are told in Proverbs 20:10, *"Divers weights, and divers measures, both of them are alike abomination to the LORD."* and Proverbs 19:5 states, *"A false witness shall not be unpunished, and he that speaketh lies shall not escape."*

The philosopher Friedrich Nietzsche's anti-democratic, anti-Christian, and anti-Semitic philosophies became popular in Europe during the 1900s and permeated American college campuses during the 1960s.

His rebellion against the "institutions" which curbed his paganistic views gave the forces of evil, permission to propagate shockingly arrogant rebellion against—the God Who was widely acknowledged to be the true Savior of mankind. It was Nietzsche's writings and proclamation: "God is dead" that set the tone for the modern age of permissive and deliberate invention of individual truth. Alfred Kinsey's cynical twisting of truth was rooted in Nietzsche and Freud's 'Oedipus Complex,' and contributed greatly to the present-day chain of distorted thought.

We can see in these revelations, the corruption of the message spoken by John the Baptist in John 3:30, *"He must increase, but I must decrease"* which opposes the corrupt viewpoint, "God is dead." Is not the logical result of such a bastardization of truth, not self-aggrandizement, and brutal self-service in rape, sadism, and murder? Many have followed this twisted path. Unfortunately, Nietzsche has been the single greatest intellectual influence on academia, politics, and ethics today. Nietzsche made pathological narcissism respectable to intellectuals who filled the classrooms during the1960s and 70s—we are much poorer for it today.

(Madison721@aol.com,AOLFriedrichNietzsche—Existentialism, www.age-of-the-sage.org/philosophy/nietzsche.html)

> *"Son of man, I have made thee a watchman unto the house of Israel: therefore, hear the word at my mouth, and give them warning from me. When I say unto the wicked, Thou shalt surely die; and thou givest him not warning, nor speakest to warn the wicked from his wicked way, to save his life; the same wicked man shall die in his iniquity; but his blood will I require at thine hand. Yet if thou warn the wicked, and he turn not from his wickedness, nor from his wicked way, he shall die in his iniquity; but thou hast delivered thy soul."* —Ezekiel 3: 17-19

Our job is not to sit in judgment but rather to know the "will of God" which is truth, and to speak that truth in love. If we are seen as "mean-spirited," then there is something wrong with how we are speaking the truth. We are to speak the truth because we love people enough to care about their souls, not because we hate them for their actions. We seek the heart of God and the mind of Christ, which will lead us while speaking the truth in such a way that the person knows the consequences of his sin.

BIBLICAL REFLECTIONS

Psalm 5:6—*"Thou shalt destroy them that speak leasing: the LORD will abhor the bloody and deceitful man."*

Psalm 34:13—*"Keep thy tongue from evil, and thy lips from speaking guile."*

Proverbs 20:11—*"Even a child is known by his doings, whether his work be pure, and whether it be right."*

DEFENSE MECHANISMS: WALLS WE BUILD

Isaiah 59:4—*"None calleth for justice, nor any pleadeth for truth: they trust in vanity, and speak lies; they conceive mischief, and bring forth iniquity."*

When a young child spills his glass of milk, he is as amazed as everyone else. When he sees his milk suddenly flowing over the table and onto the floor, he becomes startled and does not know what to do. The way his parents or caretaker deal with this situation will teach the child how to solve the problem.

> **There are as many defenses as there are situations**

If it is casually cleaned up in a matter-of-fact, "accidents-do-happen" manner, the child learns to handle his next mishap calmly. On the other hand, if they rant and rave about the terrible mess he made, spank him, and send him to his room; he may see himself as being bad. He may also see himself as the cause of his parent's anger. Immediately, the lies take root—"I'm to blame for my parent's anger." "When they get angry, bad things happen, and it hurts." "Therefore, I must not make Mom and Dad angry." The next time the child has an accident, he immediately begins to protect himself from the wrath of his parents. He may put his hand over his head and say, "I'm sorry, I'm sorry," or he may say, "I didn't do it!" Everyone saw him do it, but that does not matter to him. The main thing is to avoid the pain of his parent's disapproval.

It is not so strange that after years of lying to defend himself, now a grown adult faced with something serious like an auto accident; raises his hands to his head and says, "I didn't do it, I didn't do it." If we could look at each defense mechanism, we would find a lie embedded at the very root of each defense mechanism. Look at these examples of defense mechanisms and find some you can relate to:

Blaming: "It's all his fault."
The Lie: "Mistakes or accidents are not tolerated; I must not let them know I did this."

People Pleasing: "Sure, I can lend you $500."
The Lie: "I must do whatever you want me to do to get you to like me."

Lying: "I didn't hear him say anything."
The Lie: "If I tell the truth, I'll make him hate me. I couldn't stand that."

Rationalizing: "Aw, I did okay. Everybody got bad grades. Only the teacher's pets passed."
The Lie: "I can't tell anyone I failed. It would be too shameful."
Withdrawal: "I'm not feeling well, so I'm not going to the party."
The Lie: "I can't face those people because they'll think I'm fat and ugly."

Acquiescing: "Yeah, I guess I could go if my mom and ad will let me."
The Lie: "I don't have the right to say "no."

Attacking: "I'll bust you in the nose if you come close."
The Lie: "I can't trust anyone, so I won't let you get close to me. You'll hurt me like all the others."

<u>Getting High:</u> "I can't handle this anymore. I need a drink."
<u>The Lie:</u> "I am more effective after a drink (or a joint, etc.)."

<u>Put Downs:</u> "Oh, you're so stupid. Who's going to listen to you!"
<u>The Lie:</u> "If I put you down, it will make me feel more important."

There are as many defenses as there are situations. All of us have experienced them. Look at the following list of common defense mechanisms and see which of these defenses you find yourself using. The following is taken from *The Lies We Believe* by Chris Thurman.

DEFENSE MECHANISMS
Author: Dr. Chris Thurman, Psychologist, Thomas Nelson Publishing

Alienating: Pushing other people away to avoid being confronted with reality

Anger: A secondary feeling that is used to cover the primary (or true) feeling

Attacking: Is usually a form of anger and the act of putting onto someone else or something else what actually belongs to you

Being Obnoxious: A method used to push others away, or to manipulate them in order to avoid dealing with reality

Being Reckless: A form of endangering self-and/or others to avoid dealing with the true problem

Blaming: Not accepting responsibility or not putting responsibility where it belongs

Changing Subject: A method of changing the focus to avoid the problem

Cheating: Avoiding work, pain and/or responsibility; the act of *"looking for an easier and/or softer way"* of obtaining something

Crying: Using tears to avoid dealing with the true problem or conflict—also can be used to get someone to back off

Cussing: Foul language used to avoid the true issue

Denial: Telling oneself it has not happened

Destruction: Harmful tactics or methods used against an object, an animal, or another person as an outlet for the true problem; a negative, angry way of acting out

Excusing: Providing an alibi or a reason for behavior even when aware of the truth

Explaining: The act of giving reasons for behavior to avoid self-responsibility—behavior is irrational (justifying inappropriate behavior)

Flattery: Over-complimenting a person to get something in return

Generalizing: Skirting the issue to avoid addressing specific aspects of a problem

Getting High: Using alcohol or drugs to avoid or reject reality

Hiding: A form of self-imposed isolation used to avoid self-responsibility by escaping the true situation, problem or conflict

Hitting: A physical attack used to avoid self-responsibility for, or to divert attention from the true problem, conflict, or situation

Hostility: A self-defense mode of anger/aggression used to protect oneself against a perceived threat

Humor: Making light of or making a joke of something that is serious

Ignoring: The refusal to recognize or acknowledge an existence or reality in order to avoid a problem, a situation or responsibility

Intellectualizing: The use of scientific reasoning to justify behavior and to avoid responsibility. Use of lengthy argument or a small detail to distract from the task at hand. Attending to an issue or problem on a cognitive level to avoid "feeling" and emotional discomfort

Isolating: The act of sealing off the outside world to avoid dealing with the truth, a problem or conflict

Justifying: The act of giving reasons to make a "wrong" a "right" and to avoid self-responsibility

Lying: Rejection of the whole truth or part of the truth in order to avoid self-responsibility

Manipulating: Using coercion to have one's needs met instead of making a direct request

Maximizing: The act of making something bigger or more important than it is. *"Blowing it out of proportion"* to gain sympathy or attention

Minimizing: The act of making something smaller or less important than it is, usually to avoid embarrassment or punishment

Not Listening: Tuning out by not acknowledging another person's message. Rejecting or avoiding the whole truth or part of the truth

Passiveness: Withdrawal used to avoid self-responsibility in a situation or a conflict

People Pleasing: The act of saying or doing what you think others want to hear or see. The goal n people pleasing is to get others to like you and to avoid self- responsibility

Put-Downs: Derogatory comments to degrade another person so that you may avoid attending to what they are saying

Rationalizing: Making the assumption that because *"A"* is true, and *"B"* is true, then *"C"* must also be true

Resentment: The act of holding grudges avoiding responsibility for the true problem or feeling

Running Away: Physically removing oneself from a conflict or problem in order to avoid confrontation or responsibility in dealing with the issue; used as a *"geographical"* cure

Sarcasm: Saying the opposite of what you really mean either with anger or humor

Self-Depreciation: The act of putting yourself down to avoid taking responsibility

Self-Destruction: Threatening to, or endangering self in order to avoid the true problem

Self-Pity: The act of feeling sorry for oneself as a way of avoiding self-responsibility and/or self-treatment. (i.e., "If I'm hurt, sick, tired, busy, etc., then you can't expect me to do _____."

Sex: Sexual interaction used as a defense to avoid reality, or to change the way you are feeling

Silent Treatment: Passive/aggressive behavior, which is used to avoid self-responsibility and to punish the other person in an effort to convince them to take responsibility

Smiling: A physical response used to cover the true feeling or response

Squealing: Telling something about someone else in order to take the focus off yourself and put it onto someone else

Stealing: An "easier, softer way" of getting what you want without taking the self-responsibility for the work needed to obtain it, or to avoid confrontation

Story Telling: A form of explaining that hides the important facts of a situation or problem by using irrelevant information or statements

Sulking: A form of withdrawal used to avoid self-responsibility and to draw attention to oneself

Threatening: Attacking to get someone to back off a sensitive issue

Vandalism: Destructive acts used to avoid dealing with the real situation or conflict

Withdrawal: Removing oneself physically, mentally, or emotionally from a situation, problem or conflict in order to avoid self-responsibility

Yelling: Loud, aggressive, verbal attacking used to avoid dealing with the true problem or conflict; may be used to get someone to back away

(Source: Dr. Chris Thurman, The Lies We Believe, *2002 by Thomas Nelson)*

Again, there are as many defenses as there are situations because our human pride is so deceiving. We aren't even aware of the depth to which we will stoop to protect *SELF*. Our sinful nature is so much a part of us that we lie and cover up even when it is not necessary. The only thing that breaks that pattern is to know and experience the grace of God. God will deliberately put us in situations where our pride and humility will be tested. Remember, we can hide nothing from Him. He knows our every fault and flaw, our every thought and desire. Yet, we think we can deceive Him because we deceive people. While we live in these bodies, we will struggle with the flesh.

People do not realize they are turning their backs on God when they employ these control mechanisms. They play when they should work, work when they should rest, and rest when they should pray.

We also turn our backs on God—becoming wild and willful, impertinent and arrogant, clever and crafty, frightened, and filled with lies. Even the small, wounded ones of us who need a gentle hand turn our backs on God by playing in the fields of our minds, seeking the comfort of our fantasies, and doing anything we can do to avoid facing our issues.

We, though wounded, need to be held accountable and taught the value of discipline. We need a balance of love and discipline; grace and justice. Too few Christians understand the principle of discipline as spoken of in Hebrews 12. Discipline today is seen as punishment. The authority of parents and leaders has been undermined by our rebellion against the authority of God. We do not want to be denied anything we desire. We must realize that God's plan is for a disciplined life—a life of balance between work and rest; love and discipline. He is our stabilizer, our rock to whom we cling in the storms of life.

"My son, despise not thou the chastening of the Lord, nor faint when thou art rebuked of him: For whom the Lord loveth he chasteneth, and scourgeth every son whom he receiveth. If ye endure chastening, God dealeth with you as with sons; for what son is he whom the father chasteneth not? But if ye be without chastisement, whereof all are partakers, then are ye bastards, and not sons. Furthermor, we have had fathers of our flesh which corrected us, and we gave them reverence: shall we not much rather be in subjection unto the Father of spirits, and live? For they verily for a few days chastened us after their own pleasure; but he for our profit, that we might be partakers of his holiness.1 Now no chastening for the present seemeth to be joyous, but grievous: nevertheless afterward it yieldeth the peaceable fruit of righteousness unto them which are exercised thereby. Wherefore lift up the hands which hang down, and the feeble knees; And make straight paths for your feet, lest that which is lame be turned out of the way; but let it rather be healed." —Hebrews 12:5b-13

Discipline provides boundaries within which we can operate. Within those boundaries, we experience freedom, joy, and peace for ourselves. At the same time, we also learn to respect the boundaries of others which allows them to experience the same freedom, joy, and peace as we do.

 **REFLECTIVE EXERCISE**

What defense mechanisms do you recognize in your own life?

_____
_____
_____

Why do you think you have used those particular defense mechanisms?

_____
_____
_____

Imagine each defense mechanism is like a brick in a wall you built to defend yourself. Now imagine taking that brick from the wall and renouncing the lie behind each *Defense Mechanism*. Ask for forgiveness and replace the lie with God's TRUTH. Visualize yourself creating a path with the same bricks that you once used to build walls, but NOW leads to the CROSS OF SALVATION—lay that life down at the time of repentance. As we lay down our sins, we are forgiven and receive newness of life—forming a path that leads to life in the Spirit.

BIBLICAL REFLECTIONS

II Corinthians 4:7-12— *"But we have this treasure in earthen vessels, that the excellency of the power may be of God, and not of us. We are troubled on every side, yet not distressed; we are perplexed, but not in despair; Persecuted, but not forsaken; cast down, but not destroyed; Always bearing about in the body the dying of the Lord Jesus, that the life also of Jesus might be made manifest in our body. For we which live are always delivered unto death for Jesus' sake, that the life also of Jesus might be made manifest in our mortal flesh. So then death worketh in us, but life in you."*

Romans 15:13—*"Now the God of hope fill you with all joy and peace in believing, that ye may abound in hope, through the power of the Holy Ghost."*

Prayer to Break the Power of Lies

Father God,
In the name of Jesus Christ, my Lord, I renounce the lie of the devil who would have me believe (identify the lie) _____. These lies have caused me to build defenses to protect myself. You have shown me the truth, and the truth is _____.
I release the control I felt I needed to have—to protect myself, and I choose to tear down that wall, today. I choose to walk in truth from this day forward. I break the power of this lie and defensiveness over my life. I renounce the Spirit of lies and deception. I now choose to walk in the truth which sets me free from bondage. I claim freedom right now in Jesus' name. Amen

Lesson Nine

WEB OF LIES

Lesson Nine

Web of Lies

SOWING AND REAPING

There is a biblical principle that underscores every act of man—*every word and every deed will reap good or reap evil.* Every action has a reaction and a consequence, whether good or evil. These are all based on the motivation of the heart. Study the following scriptures to understand God's thorough plan. When God created the world, He ordained that every function is interactive with its surrounding functions. Nothing stands alone in God's scheme of things. In the book of Matthew, we learn this principle from Jesus—*"Either make the tree good, and his fruit good; or else make the tree corrupt, and his fruit corrupt: for the tree is known by his fruit."*—Matthew 12:33

"Be not deceived; God is not mocked: for whatsoever a man soweth, that shall he also reap. For he that soweth to his flesh shall of the flesh reap corruption; but he that soweth to the Spirit shall of the Spirit reap life everlasting. And let us not be weary in well doing: for in due season we shall reap, if we faint not." —Galatians 6:7-9

"A false witness shall not be unpunished, and he that speaketh lies shall not escape." —Proverbs 19:5

"Sow to yourselves in righteousness, reap in mercy; break up your fallow ground: for it is time to seek the LORD, till he come and rain righteousness upon you." —Hosea 10:12

 **REFLECTIVE EXERCISE**

Write your understanding of the biblical principle of sowing and reaping from the scriptures listed above.

_____
_____
_____

Identify results from the theory of *sowing* and *reaping* in your personal life and/or that of your family.

_____
_____
_____

"Now the serpent was more subtil than any beast of the field which the LORD God had made. And he said unto the woman, Yea, hath God said, Ye shall not eat of every tree of the garden?" —Genesis 3:1

The Lies We Believe

Most of our unhappiness and emotional struggles began in the Garden of Eden. Eve believed the lie of the serpent so did Adam. From that point on, their lives of peace and eternal life were over. We, like Adam and Eve, have believed lies from the enemy. These lies are transported in many ways from person to person through the media, television, radio, internet, newspapers, books, videos, movies, etc. Our minds may seem like a giant recording, constantly playing and replaying the messages stored in our memories, both lies, and truth. The harmful ones produce emotional misery, while the truth produces emotional health.

TYPES OF LIES WE BELIEVE

(Taken from *The Lies We Believe,* by Dr. Chris Thurman, Thomas Nelson, 2002)

1. **Self-Lies**
   - I must be perfect.
   - I must have everyone's love and approval.
   - Confrontation brings pain.
   - It is not safe, to be honest about my thoughts and feelings.
   - I can't be happy unless things go my way.
   - No one cares about me; therefore, I must take care of myself.
   - I'm unlovable, unworthy of love, unacceptable.

2. **Worldly Lies**
   - You can have it all—and you can have it now (instant gratification)
   - You are only as good as what you do.
   - You can and should meet all my needs.
   - You owe me.
   - I shouldn't have to change.
   - You should be like me.

3. **Marital Lies**
   - If you'd change, our marriage will be perfect.
   - If it takes hard work, we must not be right for each other.
   - You can and should meet my needs.
   - You owe me.
   - I shouldn't have to change.
   - You should be like me.

4. **Distortion Lies**
   - This is more than I can handle.
   - It's all my fault.
   - If you're right, I must be wrong. If I'm right, you must be wrong.
   - I'll never get through this. This is hopeless.
   - This always happens to me.

- I'm a failure. I can never succeed.
- Nobody likes me. My life doesn't matter.

5. **Religious Lies**
   - God's love must be earned.
   - I can never be forgiven for the terrible things I've done.
   - God hates me.
   - Since I'm a Christian, God will keep me from pain and suffering.
   - Death and suffering are bad and should never happen to anyone.
   - It's my Christian duty to meet all the needs of others.
   - A good Christian doesn't feel angry, anxious, or depressed.
   - God can't use me unless I'm spiritually strong.

REFLECTIVE EXERCISE

Re-read and reflect on the scriptures listed. Give an example of each of the five types of lies that you have believed.

1. Self Lies _____
2. Worldly Lies _____
3. Marital Lies _____
4. Distortion Lies _____
5. Religious Lies _____

"According as he hath chosen us in him before the foundation of the world, that we should be holy and without blame before him in love: Having predestinated us unto the adoption of children by Jesus Christ to himself, according to the good pleasure of his will," —Ephesians 1:4-5

God's Perception Vs. My Perception

"Our bodies are amazing creations. We are learning much more from researchers who have studied the brain and memory in the last ten years. The following information helps us to understand the complexity and marvelous creation of the human brain," as stated in the book, *"Other Altars"* by Craig Lockwood, Compcare Publishers, 1993.

- When we retrieve a memory, we reactivate a whole neutral-net configuration similar to that which was activated at the time of encoding. The hippocampus (area of the brain essential for memory and learning) not only encodes this neutral-net configuration or activation profile but reinstates it when a memory is being retrieved.
- Our activation-profile process of categorizing memory is a form of "schematization" or making "schema"—generalizations of repeated sensory impressions or perceptions that come from repeated experiences.
- Schema, in turn, influences the conceptualization of data stored as memory. A person who has ten experiences of picking up a hot pan does not remember each of the other ten times; he simply produces a schema for it.

Our brains first take in sensory stimuli by focusing on certain aspects of stimuli then form memories, and generalize those memories into mental models or schema. At approximately age five, the brain develops the ability to form its representations in a neutral-activation profile; resulting in the appearance-reality distinction.

Our perspective of what happened is the information we have to work with, while other pieces of the story may come into place as others tell how they saw it. We are all familiar with this game or exercise: a group of individuals is blindfolded and asked to describe what they are touching.

The object is an elephant; each touches a different part of the elephant—one individual touches the trunk, another a leg, another an ear, and another touches the tusk, etc. Each individual has a different perception of the object.

This is also true with any accident or traumatic situation. Seeing the situation from our perspective can rule our emotions and stir up all kinds of problems because our perceptions are influenced by the bitter roots and lies of the enemy. We record our feelings about each situation/incident—how we felt about how the situation was handled and how our pain or trauma was treated. Along with each puzzle piece of memory, seeds of lies are planted by the enemy in our minds—"It's all your fault," "If you had not told her she could go, this would not have happened," or "If I tell them the truth, they'll never forgive me."

REFLECTIVE EXERCISE

Review the following chart and identify your misperceptions. The Chart is entitled "God's Perception Vs. My Perception" and is located on the following page. Look up the scripture references and write them down. Practice renouncing the lies you believed and replace them with God's TRUTH.

	My Perception	God's Perception	Scripture
1.	I am unworthy/unacceptable.	I am worthy/accepted.	Romans 15:7; Psalm 139
2.	I am alone.	I am never alone.	Hebrews 13:5 b Romans 8:38-39
3.	I feel like a failure/inadequate.	I am adequate.	II Corinthians 3:5-6 Philippians 4:13
4.	I have no confidence.	I have all the boldness/confidence I need.	Proverbs 3:26; 14:26 Ephesians 3:12
5.	I feel completely responsible for everything in my life.	God is responsible/faithful to me.	Philippians 1:6; 2:13 II Thessalonians 3:3 Psalm 138:8
6.	I am confused/think I am going crazy.	I have the mind of Christ.	I Corinthians 2:16 II Timothy 1:7
7.	I am depressed/hopeless.	I have all the hope I need.	Romans 15:13 Psalm 16.11, 27:13, 31:24
8.	I am not good enough/imperfect.	I am made perfect in Christ.	Hebrews 10:14 Colossians 2:13
9.	There is nothing special about me.	I have been chosen/set apart by God.	Psalm 139 I Corinthians 1:30, 6:11 Ephesians 1:4 Hebrews 10:10, 14
10.	I don't have enough.	I have no lack.	Philippians 4:19
11.	I am fearful/anxious.	I am free from fear.	Psalm 34:4, II Timothy 1:7, I Peter 5; I John 4:18
12.	I lack faith.	I have all the faith I need.	Romans 12:3
13.	I am a weak person.	I am strong in Christ.	Daniel 11:32; Psalm 37:34 Philippians 4
14.	I am defeated.	I am victorious.	Romans 8:37 II Corinthians 2:14 I John 5:4
15.	I am not very smart.	I have God's wisdom.	Proverbs 2:6-7 I Corinthians 1:30
16.	I am in bondage.	I am free in Christ.	Psalm 32:7; John 8:36 II Corinthians 1:30
17.	I am miserable.	I have God's comfort.	John 15:6, 16:7 II Corinthians 1:3-4
18.	I have no one to take care of me.	I am protected/safe.	Psalm 32:7
19.	I am unloved.	I am very loved.	John 15:9

God's Perception Vs. My Perception

MEMORIES HOLD LIES

Our memories whether good or bad hold truth, but they may also hold lies. Looking back at our lives, our memories of what happened may be distorted or colored by our perception. An angry daddy may seem like a fierce bear to a tiny tot—when daddy just raised his voice. Nonetheless, fear struck at the heart of the little tot, and he gained a fear of Daddy. A mother who didn't have time for her first child because a new baby came prematurely—having many needs, may cause feelings of abandonment, fear, or rejection in the older child. These memories may continually conjure up these feelings each time the child experiences the same type of activity. The spirit of fear, rejection, or abandonment is now seeded in that memory. And that memory can be transferred to other types of events that simulate fear, rejection, or abandonment.

Guardian lies are designed to keep us from remembering things we do not want to believe as being true because every child wants to love, adore, and believe in his or her parents. A child may not be able to face the truth about a parent being an alcoholic because of a guardian lie—"The kids won't have anything to do with me if I tell them my mommy is drunk all the time." This child can build up a whole fantasy about his life with mommy, deceiving himself of the truth. The lie can keep the child from dealing with the truth—"Mommy is an alcoholic." It is less painful, thus easier to believe the lie rather than the truth.

Victims of abuse, whether physical, verbal, sexual, psychological, or emotional have many lies. These lies are the roots of much pain, bitterness, unforgiveness, hatred, revenge, helplessness, and hopelessness. We see the signs of abuse in the victims' physical demeanor and in their interaction with others as well as how they talk about themselves. The enemy is a liar and most of his battles are strategic—destroying God's truth. In the book; _Ishbane's Conspiracy_ by Randy Alcorn, he identifies many strategies of Satan to deceive God's people.

Listed below are a few of Satan's lies which he uses to trick people into believing:
- Get them to give in to current trends, popular opinion, and peer pressure.
- Desensitize them through movies that make entertainment with horror, blood, violence, and sex; especially let them see God's word mocked and ridiculed.
- Expose them to unrestrained sexual indulgence. Convince them that free sex leads to increased health, creativity, intelligence, and inner peace; not confusion, depression, suicide, sexually transmitted diseases, and death.
- Convince them they can live however they choose if they don't hurt anyone, and that it beats Christianity with all those rules.
- Re-define the family—Take both parents out of the home by convincing them they need two incomes. Make single parenting normal. Let the television and the internet be the babysitter and keep them away from the family dinner table.
- Keep them busy or use the telephone and television, pulling them away from the family conversation.

Lesson Ten

LIES, OATHS, & VOWS

Lesson Ten

Lies, Oaths & Vows

During our lifetime we accumulate many beliefs. Wrong beliefs are the enemy's way of weighing us down, so we can't move freely in the will of God. Many people are laden with lies that become such a burden, to the point they are always walking around under a heavy load of guilt and shame.

CARRIE'S STORY

Carrie was in her fourth year of trying one drug treatment program after another. While getting personal counseling, group therapy, and working on several programs, no one had been able to truly get in touch with the root of her drug dependency. Recognizing that drugs and alcohol are often used to numb the pain of abuse. And having been told by Carrie that she had experienced sexual abuse by her uncle at age eight, I questioned her about what else was going on in her life at that age. The one thing she remembered was that the uncle continued to molest her, and by the age of fourteen, she became sexually active. Her older sisters went to bars and "had fun" so she went with them. Then at the age of seventeen, Carrie left home to live with her drug-addicted older brother who eventually, died of a drug overdose. She was labeled as being "rebellious" for having said that she didn't like Mom and Dad's strict rules. But in reality, she was only seeking release from the pain of her loss and inability to console herself.

This is Carrie's fourth year of therapy. While meeting with Carrie and her mother, Carrie said "I didn't just wake up one morning and decide to become a drug addict." Seeking further understanding, I asked what else was going on in Carrie's life during the time of her sexual abuse. Her mother exposed that she and her husband had separated during that time, and Carrie admitted to her mother that her uncle had continued to sexually abuse her. Carrie also admitted that she became sexually active during the time Mom and Dad were separated. She remembered the grief experienced when she found her dad with his girlfriend. She also wept deeply when she remembered finding her mother in a deep depression, and couldn't awaken her. Carrie's life had fallen apart in a few short months, and she had no way to put it back together again.

God tells us in II Corinthians 4:6, *"For God, who commanded the light to shine out of darkness, hath shined in our hearts, to give the light of the knowledge of the glory of God in the face of Jesus Christ."*

Her mother until the time of our counseling, had only seen a stubborn, rebellious, and drug-addicted daughter who had brought her family through more trials than they could afford financially, physically, and emotionally. Her mother went home that night with a new understanding of her daughter, and her daughter now understood how she got to that place in her life—Carrier was even more determined to get well. God was able to shed His light on the situation and help Carrie and her mother "Get to the root of it all."

If we are going to move beyond our past negative experiences, we must recognize that our brains are created in such a way that they can be renewed. The hippocampus is located in each temporal lobe of the Limbic system of the brain; and has a curved shape resembling the skeleton of a sea horse. It is the hippocampus that holds our thoughts until we decide that they are insignificant, and should be released or stored. There is a tie between the hippocampus (the center of emotion, memory, and the autonomic nervous system), and between our thoughts, feelings, and behavior.

For example, if a fearful, traumatic, or stressful event happens enough times, in which the event holds emotion or passion as well as purpose—it goes through our hippocampus and is stored in our long-term memory. When we are faced with current events which resemble the traumatic or stressful event initially experienced, we often react to the current event the same way we reacted to the initial event. The thoughts and feelings we had during the initial event cause us to sometimes behave likewise—even if the original event happened when we were children.

We studied earlier how memories hold truth and also hold lies. We have discovered that it is not necessarily the event that creates the emotional pain for us, but rather what we have told ourselves, or what we have been told by others—possibly a lie and not the truth. For example, "You made me do it." "It's your fault." "You are stupid" are statements that represent some of those lies. When we ask Jesus to reveal the root cause of our pain or discomfort which is the lie embedded in the original memory, He will reveal it to us. He will show us the exact situation that first brought about our painful feelings. Choosing not to look at the feelings, thoughts, and emotions which are all connected to the initial event, only prolongs the healing process.

If we follow the emotion which we are currently feeling, the Lord will take us to the original memory. He will also reveal the lie we have been believing about ourselves because the lie is embedded in the wound. The lie may be spoken over us, or it may be something we assume, or we take upon ourselves e.g., "It's all my fault, I made them angry, or I made them cry." As children, we do not realize that we can't "make" people feel certain ways about us because each person is responsible for their thoughts, feelings, actions, or behaviors.

BIBLICAL REFLECTIONS
I John 2:21—*"I have not written unto you because ye know not the truth, but because ye know it, and that no lie is of the truth."*

Romans 1:25—*"Who changed the truth of God into a lie, and worshipped and served the creature more than the Creator, who is blessed for ever. Amen."*

Isaiah 28:15—*".... for we have made lies our refuge, and under falsehood have we hid ourselves:"*

Psalm 120:2—*"Deliver my soul, O LORD, from lying lips, and from a deceitful tongue."*

RENOUNCING OATHS AND VOWS
Proverbs 20:2—*"It is a snare to the man who devoureth that which is holy, and after vows to make enquiry."*

James 3:8—*"But the tongue can no man tame; it is an unruly evil, full of deadly poison."*

So, it is with human beings. The things we say are too often said without thought. Our tongues are but a small part of our body, yet the words spoken can get us into "big" trouble. The book of James has a lot to say about the tongue and its problems. Consider the following four verses:

James 3:4-6—*"Behold also the ships, which though they be so great, and are driven of fierce winds, yet are they turned about with a very small helm, whithersoever the governor listeth. Even so, the tongue is a little member, and boasteth great things. Behold, how great a matter a little fire kindleth! And the tongue is a fire, a world of iniquity: so is the tongue among our members, that it defileth the whole body, and setteth on fire the course of nature; and it is set on fire of hell."*

James 3:10—*"Out of the same mouth proceedeth blessing and cursing. My brethren, these things ought not so to be."*

When we are angry, bitter, revengeful, envious, or jealous—our words reveal our true feelings. We can say hurtful, even evil things in the heat of anger. We can also say hurtful and evil things when we are filled with hate or envy. A song from the 1960s says that "words are just words." That is like saying, "Sticks and stones may break my bones, but words will never hurt me." But of course, hurtful words do hurt! As Matthew 12:34 states, *"…. for out of the abundance of the heart the mouth speaketh."* So, words aren't *just* words, but rather they are the way someone really feels, and sometimes that hurts!

> **Words have the tremendous power to destroy.**

We have all felt the power of encouraging words, and the defeat that follows from words of criticism. We can numb ourselves from words so they don't hurt us, but to do that we must build a shell of protection around ourselves. Even though it does sometimes help to toughen up because we can't let everything devastate us, words spoken over us starting at the time of birth can direct our lives. Even the tone of voice and the actions that come from words speak volumes to us.

Words spoken over us can be meant for good or evil. Without realizing it, sometimes we play into the hands of the enemy by doing exactly what he wanted us to do. For example, the person who is abused by a parent may choose to make the following vow by saying to himself, "I'll never give them the privilege of being what they want me to be." This vow will first lead to rebellion and then to choices that will lead the person away from all authority; taking on the authority to do things their way.

On the other hand, a different child in the same situation of abuse may decide, "I am going to live." "I will never let them kill my spirit." "I will be obedient, but I will also trust God to provide a way for me to live." The second child tapped into hope rather than despair and never gave up on the hope of becoming all that God wanted him to be. The first child gave in to his weak flesh, thus giving the enemy what he wanted—death. We usually stand on our spoken word, but many times we are standing on inner vows and oaths of which we aren't even aware. Sometimes our inner vows defeat us and become counter-productive to what we want to do in life.

A man's word, was at one time something to be valued because he was "true to his word," and he was known for "keeping his word." Every contract and agreement act as an agreement to keep our "word," or a promise to keep our "word." How many times would we like to "eat our words" because our words are spoken out of haste? In the book of Numbers, we are told that God takes vows and oaths seriously.

BIBLICAL REFLECTIONS
Renouncing Oaths and Vows

Hosea 10:4—*"They have spoken words, swearing falsely in making a covenant: thus judgment springeth up as hemlock in the furrows of the field."*

Psalm 61:5—*"For thou, O God, hast heard my vows: thou hast given me the heritage of those that fear thy name."*

Matthew 5:33—*"Again, ye have heard that it hath been said by them of old time, Thou shalt not forswear thyself, but shalt perform unto the Lord thine oaths:"*

INNER VOWS—PROMISES WE MAKE WITH OURSELVES

"It is a snare to the man who devoureth that which is holy, and after vows to make enquiry." —Proverbs 20:25

The vows we make with ourselves are like covenants we make with our inner self; often spoken during times when we are hurting and in pain. We have made these vows secretly; yes, promises made secretly only to ourselves and are seldomly voiced aloud. For instance, if we have a painful fight with a very close friend we may vow, "Never to speak to that friend again," or we may vow, "Never to let anyone get close to us again." If, as a child, we have been particularly wounded by a female or male, we may make an inner vow, "Never to trust persons of that sex again."

Other examples of inner vows that we may make are:
- "I am never going to have children."
- "I will never tell the truth again."
- "I will not hurt people's feelings because they may reject me."
- "I will never get married."
- "I hate men. I will never let myself get close to a man again."
- "I will never let them know what I am thinking again."

There are also other kinds of spoken words that are spoken by someone other than ourselves which bring curses over us. For instance, someone telling us that we are stupid and will never amount to anything—this statement becomes a curse over us.

God's Word tells us in Psalm 51:17, that He honors a broken and contrite heart, a heart that is full of compassion and is teachable. "A man is the measure of his word", if we do not keep our word there can be no trust. Oaths are taken seriously by God and by man, therefore a man who keeps his word is honored. Those of us who keep our word are recognized as people of integrity. Deuteronomy 29 shares an oath spoken over the Israelites who were renewing their covenant with God.

> *A man who keeps his word is honored.*

"That thou shouldest enter into covenant with the LORD thy God, and into his oath, which the LORD thy God maketh with thee this day: That he may establish thee today for a people unto himself, and that he may be unto thee a God, as he hath said unto thee, and as he hath sworn unto thy fathers, to Abraham, to Isaac, and Jacob."—Deuteronomy 29:12-13

There are times, however, in which we enter a covenant without thinking of its seriousness, and this can cause problems for us. We think we are the only one who knows about these oaths, but God is aware of every oath we have taken, and He holds us accountable.

✝

BIBLICAL REFLECTIONS
Inner Vows—Promises We Make with Ourselves

Job 22:27—*"Thou shalt make thy prayer unto him, and he shall hear thee, and thou shalt pay thy vows."*

Psalm 51:6—*"Behold, thou desirest truth in the inward parts: and in the hidden part thou shalt make me to know wisdom."*

Isaiah 19:21—*"…they shall vow a vow unto the LORD, and perform it."*

Proverbs 20:25—*"It is a snare to the man who devoureth that which is holy, and after vows to make enquiry."*

REFLECTIVE EXERCISE
Inner Vows—Promises We Make with Ourselves

In this section, you will begin to be aware of how many ways you have told yourself words that you believe; causing you to walk in ways that hinder God's work in your life. You will continue the process of healing by renouncing any inner vows you have made as the Holy Spirit reveals them to you.

List the inner vows you may have made to yourself:

_____

_____

_____

Renouncing Oaths and Vows

In this exercise, focus on the thoughtless words spoken that have guided your life as well as the lives of others. The definition of vows and oaths will help you understand the differences between the two words.

> **VOW:** Merriam-Webster Dictionary Definition
> 1. A solemn promise or assertion
> 2. A promise that binds a person to an act, service or condition
> 3. To bind or commit by a vow

Proverbs 20:25—*"It is a snare to the man who devoureth that which is holy, and after vows to make enquiry."*

Matthew 12:34—*"O generation of vipers, how can ye, being evil, speak good things? for out of the abundance of the heart the mouth speaketh."*

Matthew 15:19—*"For out of the heart proceed evil thoughts, murders, adulteries, fornications, thefts, false witness, blasphemies:"*

Proverbs 12:23—*"A prudent man concealeth knowledge: but the heart of fools proclaimeth foolishness."*

> **OATH:** Merriam-Webster Dictionary Definition
> 1. A solemn appeal to God to witness a promise
> 2. An irreverent or careless use of a sacred name
> 3. A vow as a solemn promise or assertion; especially one by which a person binds himself to an act, service, or condition

Matthew 5:33—*"Again, ye have heard that it hath been said by them of old time, Thou shalt not forswear thyself, but shalt perform unto the Lord thine oaths:"*

Psalm 61:5—*"For thou, O God, hast heard my vows: thou hast given me the heritage of those that fear thy name."*

Identify the vows and oaths you have spoken to yourself or others.

___

___

___

What lies have you believed?

___

___

___

What promises did you make to yourself as a result of the lies?

___

___

___

Prayer of Renunciation of Oaths and Vows

Dear Father,
In the name of the Lord Jesus Christ, I cancel forever all the oaths and vows I have made—those I remember and those I don't remember that are contrary to the will of my Heavenly Father. I destroy the curses and effects, thereof replacing them with the truth of your Word. I cancel every one of them and destroy by the finger of the Living God all the curses, and effects that these oaths and vows have over me or anyone else. In their place, I bless all those involved with every blessing that I can give; setting them free from all my judgments and condemnations. I bring to the cross for crucifixion all attitudes, habits, practices, and consequences coming from my inner vows, and count them dead on the cross when Christ died. I renounce the lies I believed that caused me to make these inner vows. I ask for the Light of Jesus to be shed on my path, so that I may walk in truth and light for the rest of my days. In Jesus' Name, I pray. Amen.

Lesson Eleven
Out of Darkness

Lesson Eleven

Out of Darkness

*"Search me, O God, and know my heart: try me, and know my thoughts:
And see if there be any wicked way in me, and lead me in the way everlasting."* —Psalm 139:23-24

JOHARI WINDOW

	Known to Self	Unknown to Self
Known to Others	My Public Self	My Blind Spot
Unknown to Others	My Hidden Self	My Unconscious Self

The Johari Window, named for its creators: Joseph Luft and Harry Ingham, is a valuable tool that can help us understand how to live more effective lives. There are four "panes" on the Johari Window that represent four parts of our *Self*.

Our *Public Self* is what we show others. Our *Hidden Self* is what we choose to hide. Our *Blind Spots* are the parts of us that others see but we do not see. Our *Unconscious Self* is the part of us we do not see, nor do others. We all have these four parts of self, but their respective sizes vary in each of us.

A more fully aware person understands why he acts the way he does and is genuine towards others. He is in touch with his needs, feelings, and values—his *True Self* or identity. A generally unaware person does not understand why he does the things he does and has significant *Blind Spots*. He is often on guard and less genuine with others because he has a substantial *Hidden Self* as a defense against his shame.

When we have significant pain usually from childhood, it can cause us to use whatever defenses we need to survive. Those defenses may help for a short time, but can cause problems in the long run because we often need to detach from our feelings/ *True Self;* causing us to become out of touch with who we are.

Sometimes we wonder where certain behaviors and beliefs come from, and wonder how they became so predominant.

1. Most of our dominant imprints come from our parents. The rest come from life experiences.
2. Fearful imprints program us for future fearful thought patterns and behaviors.
3. Fear of a certain subject or object is an intangible force that increases unless the thought patterns and beliefs are identified and managed. A child who has been frightened by a dog will experience the same emotions the next time he or she sees a dog—unless someone helps the child change the "fear of dogs" through a positive experience that will counteract the bad experience which created the fear.

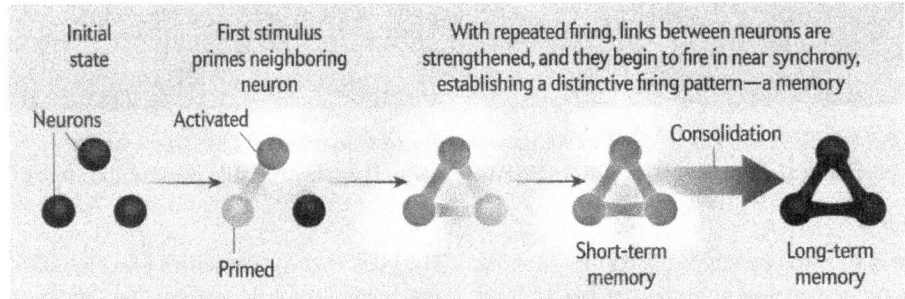

Our feelings are lodged in our hippocampus, a part of the brain that holds memories. Therefore, fears stay with us and hinder us from moving forward in our growth. The emotions we feel in situations that cause fear and panic are often triggered by stored-up emotions from experiences we have had before.

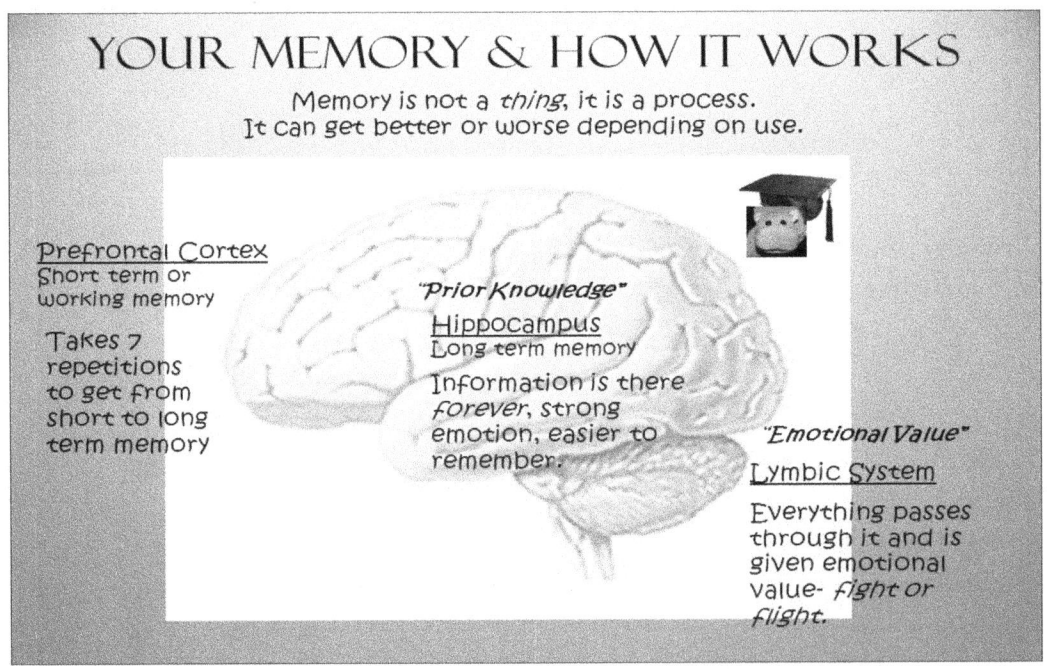

> **Emotions are often a clue to what is hidden within things we have feared to remember or discuss. We hide them so deeply inside that we forget about them until something triggers our senses, and provides an echo of the memory.**

How many of us, know ourselves well enough to be able to manage ourselves significantly to oversee our emotions? If we don't know how to control our thoughts and emotions, we will be preoccupied with them as well as the fearful emotions attached to them. If we don't manage our thoughts and emotions, so to speak "other voices" will control us. How many of us know our minds and can speak for ourselves? How many of us know what our life purpose is? Only when we are aware of our thoughts, and feelings, and can express those out loud—do we have a voice. If we do not have a voice, how will we be able to fulfill our life purpose?

> **Children do not know how to identify emotions for themselves. They have to be taught by a calm and comforting caregiver who will help the child re-experience this "life trauma" therefore transforming the child's perception of the experience. If fear goes uncontrolled, it will become a predominant controlling factor.**

REFLECTIVE EXERCISE

Take a moment to recall a few significant memories in your lifetime, both positive and negative. Try to recall your age, the location, the people involved, and any major senses that were triggered such as smells or sounds. Try to recall the emotions that memory brought with it.

_____
_____
_____
_____
_____
_____
_____
_____
_____
_____

DAN'S STORY

Dan's life was a mess until his brother encouraged him to enter the training program at the Fire Department and give it a try. After winning many awards for his heroic acts as a fireman, nearly eighteen months until retirement, he was depressed and ready to commit suicide. His "failure" to be brave and strong was more than he could handle. At fifty-five years of age, Dan came to one of our classes for prayer—so he would not do what his mind was telling him to do. Below is his *Cycle of Dysfunction* which we drew on the whiteboard that day.

PAINFUL MEMORY: A young boy was born into a family consisting of seven generations of firemen, who were considered to be strong, tough "heroes" in the eyes of their family and city. When this little boy began to demonstrate weakness or tenderness, his father would humiliate him by saying things like, "How is a sissy like you ever going to be a fireman?" "How do you expect to be a brave fireman if all you do is whine and cry?" "Come on boy! Toughen up! Firemen can't be softies!" When he displeased his father, he was yelled at. And if he did something wrong, his father would "teach him" by whipping him.

CYCLE OF DYSFUNCTION

```
        CONSEQUENCES  →  ORIGINAL EVENT
             ↑                    ↓
      FIGHT OR FLIGHT         BELIEFS
             ↖                    ↙
          GASTRO INTESTINAL AND BODILY SYMPTOMS
```

A. **BELIEFS**: Seeing himself as a weak and a soft failure who could do nothing right, he believed he would never succeed and certainly never be the eighth-generation family fireman.

B. **EMOTIONS:** By the age of five, he felt unsafe at home and was having panic attacks whenever his dad was home. He stuttered and was put into special education classes. Feeling full of fear, hate, shame, guilt, and rage, he avoided intimacy.

C. BEHAVIOR: By the age of ten, he stayed away from home; not wanting to be there whenever Dad was home, so as not to be beaten and shamed. He wandered the neighborhood, experienced rages at the drop of a hat; and became involved with drugs, alcohol, and sex.

D. CONSEQUENCES: Early childhood panic attacks, stuttering, learning disabilities, DUI, drug treatment, and pregnancy/abortion.

DIAGRAM: CYCLE OF DYSFUNCTION

If we have been taught since childhood that we are a child of God who belongs to God's family, God has a purpose for our lives, our name is written in His "Book of Life," God is with us, and He loves us—we will most likely be free to move in our gifting; flowing from developmental stage to developmental stage, without missing a beat. Those who have grown up fearing for their safety and security; believing themselves to be unwanted, unloved, and rejected—often see themselves as "being everybody's problem," "not good enough," and "a failure." Not to mention, their negative life experiences will prove repeatedly that they are unsafe and uncared for. It will be difficult for people who experience this kind of childhood to move freely through the different stages of development because they are experiencing inadequacy, insecurity, failure, etc. These feelings will eventually cause them to develop "defense mechanisms" such as explaining, withdrawing, blaming, procrastination, lying, making excuses, justifying, etc., —they are identifying with their weaknesses, rather than their strengths.

Our state of being has an infectious dominating factor that takes up residence in our minds. For example, anger and hatred will replace peace and joy, while envy and jealousy will replace generosity and trust. Anger, if given space will become a predominant state which will eventually overtake your entire being. Children will defend their lives one way or another! These defense mechanisms become a way of life until we examine them. Examining them, allows us to get to the root of the "lie" that they are based on. Below, are the defense mechanisms used by Dan.

DEFENSE MECHANISMS
(List on pages 61–64)

ALIENATION / WITHDRAWAL
ATTACKING / ACQUIESCING
BLAMING / SILENCE
PERFECTION / PROCRASTINATION
LYING / MANIPULATING
SELF-MEDICATING

REFLECTIVE EXERCISE
Reflect on Lesson 8, "Walls We Build" to re-examine your Defense Mechanisms (pgs. 61–64)

The consequences involving this cycle of thinking are physical and emotional impairments such as attachment issues, anxiety, addictions, self-regulatory problems, aggression, social helplessness, eating disorders, and re-victimization among others. These emotional problems lead to system damage such as circulatory problems, coronary artery disease, immune system diseases, Type 1 diabetes, and cancer. The price Dan paid for his trauma consisted of problems in his marriage, anxiety, addictions, self-regulatory problems, aggression, suicidal thoughts, and social helplessness. These emotional problems lead to system damage such as circulatory problems, coronary artery disease, immune system disease, etc.

MULTIPLE DOMAINS OF IMPAIRMENT
a. Self-regulatory problems, attachment issues, anxiety, affective disorders
b. Addictions
c. Aggression, social helplessness, eating disorders
d. Dissociative, cardiovascular, immunological disorders
e. Sexual disorders
f. Re-victimization

SYSTEM DAMAGE
a. Circulatory problems
b. Coronary Artery Disease
c. Immune System Diseases
d. Type 1 Diabetes
e. Cancer—when the body turns on itself instead of the disease

Our life experiences prepare us to see ourselves in one of two states: empowered or disempowered. In each event, (car accident, argument, disappointment, etc.) based on your background and programming—you will experience a thought, interpretation, and action within a micro-second.

Those who are programmed with negative thoughts and beliefs will act upon the beliefs and interpretations which they have been programmed to believe—with repetitive negative results. Those who have been programmed with love, encouragement, and truth—will feel secure in making the right choices and acting accordingly.

DISEMPOWERED

Dan saw himself as "DISEMPOWERED." He was a fireman by the age of forty-five, on September 11, 2001, Dan was called to an office building to check on a call. As he walked into the office building dozens of people were standing around a large television set watching as a plane flew into one of the Twin Towers in New York City. On September 11, 2021, two hijacked planes struck the Twin Towers of the World Trade Center and another plane destroyed the western side of the Pentagon. People were jumping out of the buildings, crying, screaming, and panicking as firemen were carrying people to safety. The firemen were fighting against the fire and smoke while trying to save lives. The people who were watching the television set in the room became hysterical at what they were witnessing. Dan sank to the floor in an absolute panic while sweat covered his face, tears filled his eyes, and his heart beat like a drum; he could hardly breathe. Dan didn't know what hit him. He went back to the office and told his boss he wanted a desk job because he could no longer handle being a firefighter. His boss considered his request, but the next day sent him out to check on a dog bite. He found a little girl who had been bitten by a dog. The dog caught her jugular vein, causing the little girl to bleed to death. He froze, unable to do anything because he couldn't pull himself out of it. He was numb and speechless. He went back to the office and told his boss again that he wanted a desk job. So, for the next ten years, Dan was working at a desk job. A man who had won many awards for his heroic acts of saving lives decided that he would just sit it out until retirement.

On the day Dan called his wife for help, she was at one of our seminars, and her big concern that day had been her husband—September 11, 2011—the tenth anniversary of 9/11—the bombing of the Twin Towers in New York. One-half hour before class was over Dan phoned his wife and said, "He was considering suicide, and asked if he would come to class if we would pray with him." We said, "Yes." When Dan arrived, we asked him to tell us what was going on. Dan responded by telling the story of his experience on September 11, 2001. When he recounted how he saw himself as a failure, his wife responded to him saying, "But you won all these awards." We asked him where he got the idea that he was a failure. Then Dan immediately recounted all of the negative ways his father had programmed him to see himself.

As I listened to Dan, one of my interns drew the *Cycle of Dysfunction* on the whiteboard. When we could see the finished cycle, we shared with Dan how his fears, shame, and panic attacks as well as his physical and emotional problems were all based upon the beliefs, he had about himself. I asked him if he would like to hear what God thought about him. He said "Yes." We prayed "God, Dan sees himself as a failure, as a weak person, ashamed of his failures, and he hates himself. Would you show Dan how you see him?" Dan listened for the voice of God, and God said to him "The reason you are a good fireman is because of your compassion." Then God said, "I like the person I created you to be." Dan broke down in tears, and his body shook with relief as every ounce of fear, stress, guilt, shame, and hatred fell off his body. His legs and body shook with relief from the released pressure of trying to be someone he was not created to be. Dan was set free that day and walked out of that room a changed man, a changed husband and father.

Renewing the mind is physiological, but it is also spiritual. God created our mind and neurological system to be interconnected in such a way that we can shift our state of mind in a heartbeat. Your response to stimuli depends upon the interpretation you give about the event. The most successful way to break out of your current state is to adjust your thoughts, which then will change your feelings. That is because your thoughts program your body to act in a certain way, and your body is programmed for your disposition so that you will automatically respond to your programming. Changing your physiology means changing your thoughts which also changes your feelings. Determining to change the way you think will change your programming, which will ultimately change your actions.

If your physiology speaks of love and caring, your actions will build relationships and pull people together. If it speaks of anger and rejection, a different message will be communicated ... such as strife and division which alienates you from others. Speak peace to your body, and your body will communicate peace, then you will change your environment. Your spirit has authority over the environment. If there is strife in a room, strife comes into you. Your state is like an influence, so you can attract or repel depending on your predominant state. For example, strife will repel peace Research has proven that we can control our thoughts and our emotions, but we must first become aware of our thoughts and feelings. Then examine and analyze them to determine which ones we desire to keep, and which need to be replaced.

Most conceptions, whether negative or positive, are built on past experiences which form our memories. Renewing our minds shouldn't be understood as the removal or changing of the memory, but rather the reinterpretation of the memory by replacing the embedded lie with the truth. Jesus knows all things and will shed His light upon the lie to disengage it and replace it with the truth. Shame and guilt are merely the emotions that match the belief we embrace. This is how the enemy keeps us in bondage to sin—by continually accusing us and bringing condemnation upon us. While we can't change the memory, we can change the lie embedded in the memory.

The hippocampus holds the incoming information until your free will accepts or rejects it. Later, when everything is over and we try to put the pieces together, we begin to examine the event. If it is too horrendous, we can consciously refuse to look at it. We repress the memory and tuck it away somewhere in our mind, so we won't have to look at it. This is called denial or compartmentalization.

The shock and pain suffered from traumatic abuse for some victims are too great for them to fathom that someone would do that. This thought process is called *denial*. Sometimes we blame ourselves, thinking we could have somehow avoided or prevented the abuse or accident from happening; leaving our shame and guilt to form a wall that won't allow us to remember.

However, sooner or later we will experience similar sights, sounds, or smells which can trigger the mental images and emotions of these experiences. For example, fear, anxiety, terror, shame, guilt, embarrassment, etc. can take us back to a painful memory in which we might re-live all the biochemical reactions and emotions.

Having a very uncomfortable feeling or a sense of caution may temporarily prevent us from connecting to the painful memory. We know that our negative feelings made us feel uncomfortable, sick, or afraid. **These senses are tapping into old buried and covered-up memories.** It may happen repeatedly without our making the connection between what we call the "situation" we are in, and the memory it is triggering —or the "Original Memory." If our reaction to our current situation seems like we are overreacting, we may be tapping into emotions and thoughts connected with what happened in the past (Original Memory). The body is connecting the two events because the hippocampus is remembering, and sending signals of caution and reservation of anger and fear to the body.

CYCLE OF ILLUMINATION

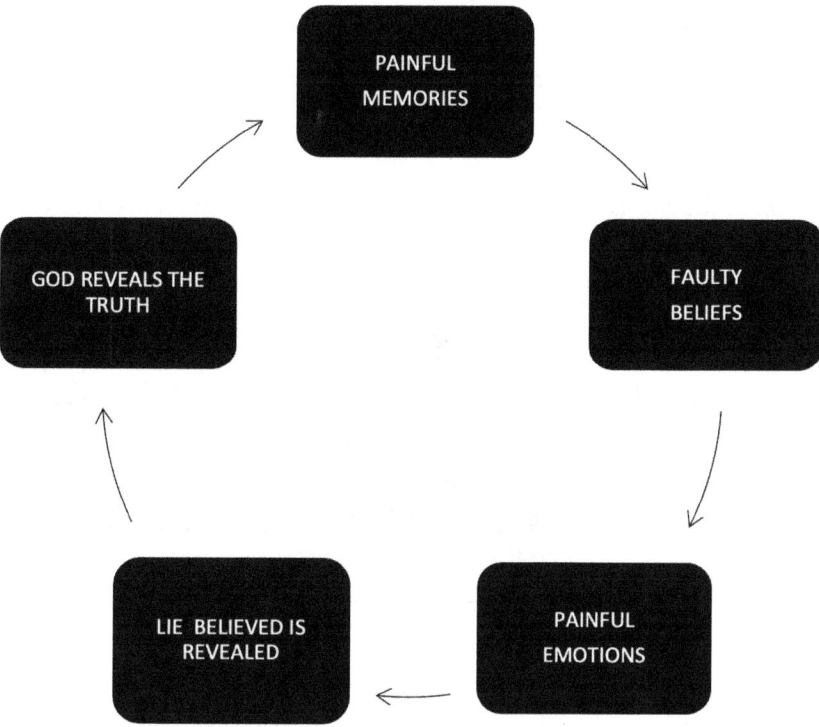

FIVE STEPS OF ILLUMINATION

1. Start with the immediate emotion. Ask the person to get in touch with the emotion they are feeling—stay with the emotion and don't run from it. (e.g., Shame)
2. Ask them, "What is the emotion telling you about yourself?" (e.g. I'm a failure)
3. Ask them to think about the first time they ever felt that way. This will usually take them back to a memory (e.g. Remembrance of being scolded for not doing something right).
4. Question: As an adult looking back on this, is it true that you were a failure? As an adult, they can now see that the judgment upon them at that time about their age was not realistic. They realize they have believed a lie (often repeated over and over in their lifetime).
5. We ask the Lord to show them the truth. (e.g., The Lord will show them that people learn from their failure.) Sometimes, God will reveal that the person scolding them was stressed by something else. He will also them to forgive those who were unreasonable in their judgment.

BIBLICAL REFLECTIONS

I Corinthians 2:10-11—*"But God hath revealed them unto us by his Spirit: for the Spirit searcheth all things, yea, the deep things of God. For what man knoweth the things of a man, save the spirit of man which is in him? Even so the things of God knoweth no man, but the Spirit of God."*

Psalms 139: 1-2—"…. *LORD, thou hast searched me, and known me. Thou knowest my downsitting and mine uprising, thou understandest my thought afar off.*"

I Corinthians 14:25—"*And thus are the secrets of his heart made manifest; and so falling down on his face he will worship God, and report that God is in you of a truth.*"

Hebrews 11:6—"*But without faith it is impossible to please him: for he that cometh to God must believe that he is and that he is a rewarder of them that diligently seek him.*"

REMEMBER....
EACH TIME GOD REVEALS A LIE AND SPEAKS THE TRUTH ABOUT IT,
THE LIE IS DISPELLED, AND THE EMOTIONAL PAIN IS HEALED.
IF MORE PAIN EXISTS, THAT IS A SIGN THERE IS MORE THAN ONE LIE INVOLVED.
REPEAT THE STEPS UNTIL ALL THE PAIN IS GONE AND YOU HAVE
COMPLETE PEACE WITH IT.

REFLECTIVE EXERCISE

Identify the elements of the *Tree of Bondage* in Dan's life and the fruit that came from that bondage:
_____
_____
_____

Identify why Dan felt un-empowered and depressed:
_____
_____
_____

Identify why our beliefs have such power over our lives:
_____
_____
_____

Diagram your *Cycle of Illumination*—Feel free to use a separate piece of paper.

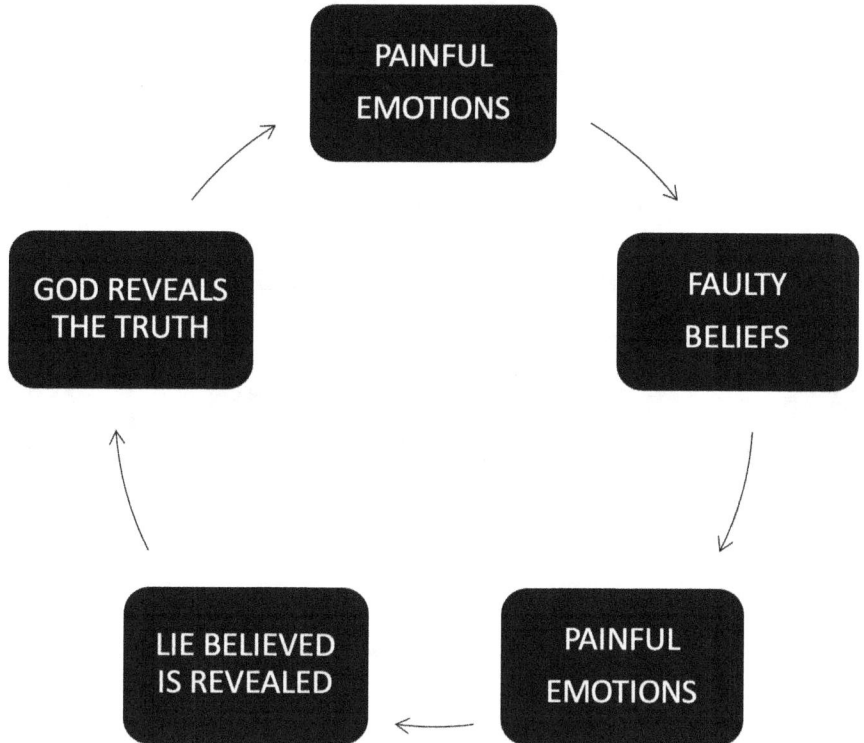

Lesson Twelve
CYCLE OF SIN & ADDICTION

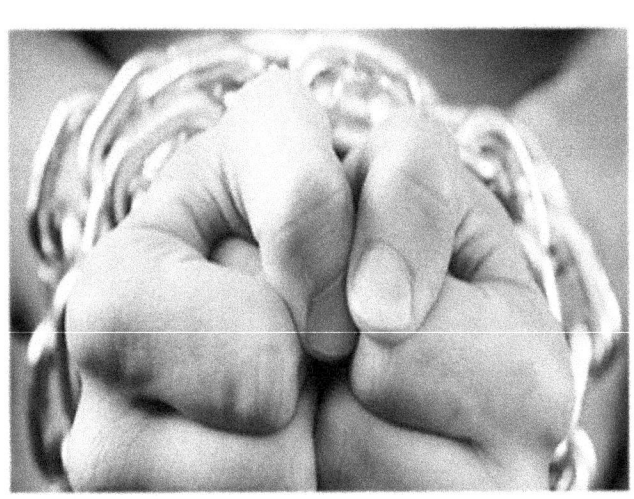

Lesson Twelve

Cycle of Sin & Addiction

THE HIDDEN EVIDENCE

"For there is nothing hid, which shall not be manifested; neither was any thing kept secret, but that it should come abroad." —Mark 4:22

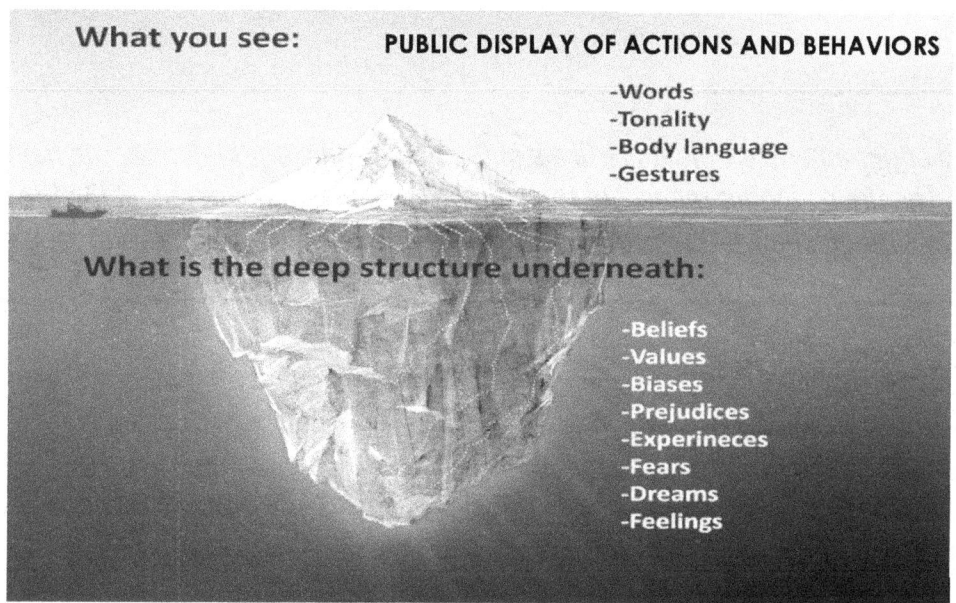

Our words and actions identify that which we allow the world to see—who we are, and how we are thinking and feel. Our verbal and body language can sometimes reveal our deeper feelings. However, some people aren't in touch with their feelings and/or emotional needs and lack the ability to express them. As caregivers, we must learn to read the underlying messages by watching non-verbal behavior. We work to detect beliefs shared through words that will give us clues regarding hidden emotional needs that are unspoken.

You may have heard the saying, "We are just seeing the tip of the iceberg." A teacher one day told of a young teenage boy who was expelled from school. The teacher had come into the classroom and found the words, "I hate you all" scrawled across three slates of blackboard. The words were written using red lipstick. When the teacher was asked, "What had caused the young man's anger?" The teacher stated that the boy didn't know. The person that asked the question responded by saying, "There has to be a reason behind such anger and hatred!" The teacher said, "Well, the student had been told the previous day that he could no longer play on the football team because of his grades." Asked if anyone had spoken to that young man regarding his anger, the teacher said, "No, that is the way things are handled." The solution to the problem was to transfer him to another school.

The tip of the iceberg is what everyone saw—the rage and hate scrawled across the blackboard. No one saw the pain caused by the disappointment and rejection due to being cast out of the group. It was from the group that the student had gained his identity and approval. The young man had not been helped to express his anger and disappointment in healthy ways, so he chose the way he knew—rage.

A young lady was in counseling because she was having problems with her job. She was also experiencing difficulties in her relationship with the young man in her life. She was feeling tremendous rejection and was also experiencing the inability to deal with her boss, who was making it difficult for her to stay in her job. As we explored, we found that the rejection she was feeling went from one situation to the other. The rejection and feelings of being unacceptable began with a negative experience she had with a basketball coach. This young lady had been on the basketball team for three of her high school years. All of her friends had been on the team with her over the years. When the coach told her, she couldn't play because she had gained too much weight over the summer, she lost her friends and her place of identification with the school. She suffered from a loss of identity and felt very much like an outcast.

> **Unresolved anger and resentment are like a still-smoldering ember left after the flames of a fire die down. The fire no longer rages, but the ember remains hot and at risk of the fire reigniting until it is extinguished. It does not take much for it to reignite, burning everyone nearby.**

As she explored further this sense of being unworthy and unacceptable, she admitted that a boy befriended her when she was cut from the basketball team. He used her for his purposes and then abused her. She didn't feel worthy enough to think someone better could love her. As she explored the lies that she believed, she dug further and the Lord revealed—even among her siblings she saw herself as "never being as good as they were." This was reinforced by the attitudes of her sisters towards her. The Lord revealed the lie, "She was not good enough." It had been manifested through this series of events.

The tip of the iceberg was—her difficulty finding her own self-worth whether at school, at work, or in the family. Beneath the water, she found deep feelings of rejection, unworthiness, and a lack of self-acceptance. These were all rooted in the lies the enemy told her from early childhood. These lies said, "Others were better than her," and "She couldn't measure up."

She overcame these lies through God's healing power and through the restoration of His Truth. She began to choose friends that reflected her values and morals rather than the ones the enemy told her she deserved. She began to claim her inheritance as a child of God; today, she is happily married and has a beautiful family.

BIBLICAL REFLECTIONS

Psalm 142:3—*"When my spirit was overwhelmed within me, then thou knewest my path. In the way wherein I walked have they privily laid a snare for me."*

Ecclesiastes 12:14—*"For God shall bring every work into judgment, with every secret thing, whether it be good, or whether it be evil."*

Jeremiah 16:17—*"For mine eyes are upon all their ways: they are not hid from my face, neither is their iniquity hid from mine eyes."*

Mark 4:22—*"For there is nothing hid, which shall not be manifested; neither was any thing kept secret, but that it should come abroad."*

II Peter 2:19—*"While they promise them liberty, they themselves are the servants of corruption: for of whom a man is overcome, of the same is he brought in bondage."*

REFLECTIVE EXERCISE
Cycle of Sin and Addiction

The consequences of defensive behaviors are usually what brings a person to the counseling room. Typically, it is in the form of depression, marital issues, unfaithfulness, sexual issues, alcohol or drug-related issues, domestic violence, parent/child problems, familial problems, etc. Each problem involves more than the individual realizes, but the problems were manifested in his life because of what lay within.

As a person tells his story, there are faulty beliefs that dictate how he responds. The reasons for going to counseling are usually due to the consequences of his chosen responses to the faulty beliefs. By the end of the first session, the client can begin to identify the cycle of sin and its consequences. He can acknowledge this to be true or false and can begin to identify the wrong behaviors which are due to his faulty beliefs. And is able to trace them to the wound brought about by his perception of life's painful events. A person can move from job to job, marriage to marriage, church to church, and still find himself repeating the same patterns of behavior. That is why it is called a cycle—people keep repeating the same mistakes until someone helps them break the cycle.

Cycles, if not broken become addictive. That person finds one way to solve his problem through dysfunctional methods and is unable to look at other options. It is like being on a train that is on a track—going round and round with nowhere to get off. Usually, by the time a person reaches the addictive stage, he can't see other alternatives.

Dysfunctional methods have always seemed to work until the consequences catch up with the person. God sends those who aren't afraid to speak the truth and are willing to lend a helping hand to those who can't break the cycle on their own.

We may have only one opportunity to speak the truth in love to people. Understanding this cycle can be a helpful tool to help us discern the cycle of sin and addiction, and to identify what needs to be done to correct the cycle in ourselves or others. Due to some of the defense mechanisms people have, the discernment may take longer than the first session. The job of the caregiver is to be able to help people see what lies beneath the surface of their problems.

BIBLICAL REFLECTIONS
Cycle of Sin and Addiction

> Cycles, if not broken, become addictive

Hebrews 4:13— *"Neither is there any creature that is not manifest in his sight: but all things are naked and opened unto the eyes of him with whom we have to do."*

Psalm 33:18— *"Behold, the eye of the LORD is upon them that fear him, upon them that hope in his mercy;"*

Zechariah 8:16— *"These are the things that ye shall do; Speak ye every man the truth to his neighbour; execute the judgment of truth and peace in your gates:"*

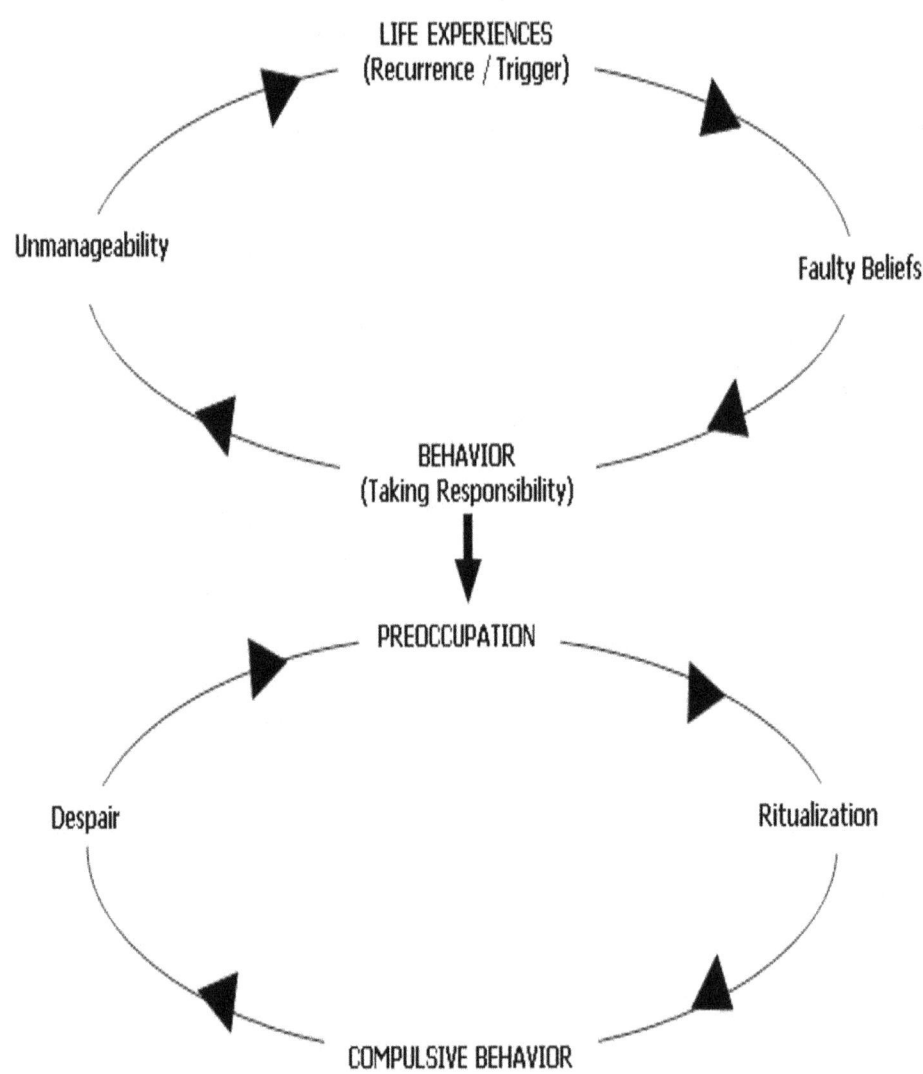

Cycle of Sin and Addiction Terms

<u>Life Experience</u>—*Original Memories* (The accumulation of all life experiences such as childhood abuse, first sexual experience, and any other event that influenced the person's perception of life).

<u>Faulty Beliefs</u>—*Original Lie* (a distorted view of self, others, and life situations e.g., "I'm to blame"). When these memories are triggered, the sensory response is called the *Memory Echo*—it is the same as the original response and is a sign that the memory has not been healed and that the lie is still embedded in the memory.

<u>Behavior</u>—*The behaviors of choice when one assumes responsibility for 'fixing the problem.'* Because issues are unresolved, these choices are made from rebellion or the need to escape. The behaviors may be in the form of drugs, alcohol, work, gambling, pornography, food, spending, displays of anger, sleeping, health problems, etc. Choices become habits; habits become addictions. These can lead to impairment in more than one area of the individual's life. (*See Defense Mechanisms* in *Chapter 8*, p. 66).

<u>Unmanageability</u>—*The result of addictive behavior.* Escaping these habits and addictions usually impairs more than one area of an individual's life including social, occupational, marital, spiritual, physical, educational, etc.

<u>Preoccupation</u>—*Compulsive fantasizing; intrusive thoughts.* The individual is focusing on the addiction ("I can't wait to do the addiction again"). It controls them instead of being in control of it.

<u>Ritualization</u>—*Routines that enhance the preoccupation with the addiction.* Habitual routines that facilitate compulsive behavior.

<u>Compulsivity</u>—*Acting out of the preoccupation* (drugs, alcohol, sex, food, television, music, work, lying, and running). Repetitiveness. Can not get it off your mind until you do it again.

<u>Despair</u>—*Feelings of guilt and hopelessness following the offense* (abuse, violence, drunkenness, rape, etc.).

(Adapted from *Out of the Shadows, Understanding Sexual Addiction* by Patrick Carnes. See appendix for listing.)

REFLECTIVE EXERCISE
Cycle of Sin and Addiction

Using an experience in your life that continues to affect you emotionally, identify the following:

- Emotion (anger, frustration, disappointment, loneliness, abandonment, rejection)

- Identify the Faulty Belief (what you believe that causes that emotion (self-talk).

- Identify how you chose to take care of your specific emotional need (silence, isolation, etc.)

- What were the consequences (loneliness, isolation, panic attack, physical problems, headaches, etc.)?

- What seems to trigger this cycle most often?

- List the choices you have made that have become a ritual, compulsion, or addiction for you (e.g. withdrawal into food, TV, internet, pornography, gambling, drugs, alcohol, spending)?

SIN LEADS TO SICKNESS AND DEATH

"Remember therefore how thou hast received and heard, and hold fast, and repent. If therefore thou shalt not watch, I will come on thee as a thief, and thou shalt not know what hour I will come upon thee." —Revelation 3:3

We do not just wake up one morning with a mental or emotional illness. Different personalities respond to life circumstances differently. As we become influenced by the times we live in and how it affects us, we often adopt the same generational patterns of survival and defense mechanisms passed down to us from our forefathers. We establish beliefs and values as we each seek and learn ways of managing the discomforts, the challenges, the trials, and the sufferings life brings our way. All these things combined influence our health and mental well-being.

Most psychoses are caused by chemical imbalances that are brought on by long-term habitual sin or stress. The body simply can't handle the effects of sin. When we worry and get anxious, when we are fearful, angry, resentful, bitter, and unforgiving, and when we dwell on the wounds of the past; we consume energy. God tells us in Psalms:

"Blessed is he whose transgression is forgiven, whose sin is covered. Blessed is the man unto whom the LORD imputeth not iniquity, and in whose spirit there is no guile. When I kept silence, my bones waxed old through my roaring all the day long. For day and night thy hand was heavy upon me: my moisture is turned into the drought of summer. Selah. I acknowledged my sin unto thee, and mine iniquity have I not hid. I said, I will confess my transgressions unto the LORD; and thou forgavest the iniquity of my sin. Selah. —Psalm 32:1-5

Our bodies suffer the consequence of all the emotional turmoil. Think of the adrenalin used when something frightens us and when we get angry and hateful. Our emotions sap us of our emotional strength, and we become physically and emotionally exhausted. We become depressed and just want to sleep. But, if we can't sleep, if we are interrupted by dreams, nightmares, musing over our hurts and pains, and worrying over our problems, our bodies are continuing to use necessary body chemicals, continually working, day and night. If this becomes a pattern for dealing with daily trials, our bodies will eventually break down in some way and stop functioning appropriately.

BIBLICAL REFLECTIONS
Sin Leads to Sickness and Death

Hebrews 3:7-8,12—*"Wherefore (as the Holy Ghost saith, To day if ye will hear his voice, Harden not your hearts, as in the provocation, in the day of temptation in the wilderness:", "Take heed, brethren, lest there be in any of you an evil heart of unbelief, in departing from the living God."*

James 1:15—*"Then when lust hath conceived, it bringeth forth sin: and sin, when it is finished, bringeth forth death."*

Romans 6:16—*"Know ye not, that to whom ye yield yourselves servants to obey, his servants ye are to whom ye obey; whether of sin unto death, or of obedience unto righteousness?"*

REFLECTIVE EXERCISE
Sin Leads to Sickness and Death

This section helps us to see that the body, mind, and spirit work together. As we go through life experiences our bodies experience the world in different ways. And our minds develop concepts and perceptions that send messages to our bodies. As stated in the text above, most psychoses or mental derangements are caused by chemical imbalances brought on by long-term habitual sin. Our bodies can't handle the effects of sin such as fear, anger, resentment, worry, bitterness, and unforgiveness. Yes, all these affect our body's chemicals and consume energy.

Identify the ways you and your family handle conflicts.
_____
_____
_____

How was anger expressed in your birth family?
_____
_____
_____

How is anger expressed in your family today?
_____
_____
_____

How were hurts and wounds handled?
_____
_____
_____

How did your family influence you positively or negatively in coping with life's struggles?
_____
_____
_____

If people do not get help in breaking this unhealthy and dysfunctional cycle, they will carry the patterns they have developed throughout their lives into every setting in which they find themselves.

Lesson Thirteen
HEALTHY BOUNDARIES

Lesson Thirteen

Healthy Boundaries

SET HEALTHY BOUNDARIES

"In the day that thy walls are to be built, in that day shall the decree be far removed." —Micah 7:11

Healthy boundaries help us feel secure because we know what is acceptable and what is not. It helps us to understand the differences between healthy and unhealthy boundaries. Healthy families put guidelines or healthy boundaries in place to protect children. When a child is a baby, he is held or laid in a bed with bumpers on all sides so that the baby won't injure his head; or get a leg or arm caught in the crib. When a child is a baby, he is held or laid in a bed with bumpers on all sides so that the baby won't injure his head; or get a leg or arm caught in the crib. When the baby becomes a toddler, to protect him from the dangers of adult activity or items on the floor, the toddler is placed in a playpen where his environment can be protected to keep the child safe. When the child gets old enough to go outside to play, the yard is usually fenced in so the child will know where his safe boundaries are located. The mother feels safe as she knows what lies within the boundaries of the fence and can remove all dangerous obstacles for the child's safety.

By the time a child goes to school, his boundaries have broadened with clear guidelines as to where he is allowed to go and how far he is allowed to go. In addition, he knows when to be home and how to get home safely. The child is taught in his formative years to express himself clearly, so his needs are met, thus learning how to take care of himself when he gets away from home.

These may seem like simple boundaries because they are for children. But many adults today who never learned they are worthy of being loved and protected. We may not know how to create "safe places" to be who God wants us to be. We do not know how to keep our environment safe. Guidance is needed.

Every abuse victim needs to take a class on setting healthy boundaries. Dr. Henry Cloud and Dr. John Townsend's books on healthy boundaries are very popular and effective.

As we described different styles of families. We learned about the concepts of boundaries earlier in lesson three: rigid, chaotic, and healthy boundaries. If we recall, boundaries are the beliefs, behaviors, values, roles, and rituals set down by the parents of the family. While each family has different boundaries, nonetheless, they have boundaries, some healthy, and some not. In these *Boundaries* books, we are guided to examine the boundaries set by our family for us and to identify how those boundaries were developed. We also learn how to develop our own set of safe boundaries for our family, friends, spouse, children, and workplace as well as for ourselves.

Listed below are some very simple, loving ways to create safe relationships:
- Teach, uphold, and practice God's laws
- Love according to I Corinthians 13
- Help people consider the consequences of their words and actions
- Help people identify the lies of the enemy
- Practice praying and confessing the Word
- Teach and model repentance and forgiveness
- Model and teach humble confessions of sins
- Provide an atmosphere of caring and compassion
- Pray with one another
- Confess God's promises over each other
- Practice the fruits of the Spirit: love, joy, peace, patience, kindness, goodness, faithfulness, gentleness, and self-control

Read the Word aloud in every room of your house

Change Unhealthy Patterns of Family Interaction
"For if a man know not how to rule his own house, how shall he take care of the church of God?" —I Timothy 3:5

It is so easy to blame God for the bad relationships we have in our families. But we all learn healthy and unhealthy ways of responding to life situations. Do we recognize that we have certain genetics that can predispose us to certain faults? Many of these predispositions have been proven to change when Jesus comes to live in our hearts.
- While there are inborn characteristics that can lead us to problems, the home environment is also crucial to the development of our relationships with our children, our spouses, our families, and our world. Many factors determine how we respond including the following:
- How your parents related to each other and to their respective families
- What was acceptable and not acceptable behavior in your family
- Your sense of adequacy and acceptance
- Your emotional maturity
- Cultural influences
- How your family handles grief
- How your family expresses love, anger
- How your family talks about finances, sex, disappointments
- How your family deals with conflict

If God can take David, the shepherd boy, and make him into a king; if He can take a greedy tax collector like Zacchaeus and turn him into a philanthropist; if He can take a cold-blooded killer like Saul and redeem him as Paul; then He can change our exceptions and reactions to our world, and thus, our behavior. With the help of the Holy Spirit, we can become one with Him, like Him in wisdom and strength.

The testimonies of people's lives are proof that Christ in us makes a dramatic difference and how much we must lay down that He may take this place in our hearts. Paul's instructions to the Ephesians continue to be good advice.

"But ye have not so learned Christ; If so be that ye have heard him, and have been taught by him, as the truth is in Jesus: That ye put off concerning the former conversation the old man, which is corrupt according to the deceitful lusts; And be renewed in the spirit of your mind; And that ye put on the new man, which after God is created in righteousness and true holiness. "Wherefore putting away lying, speak every man truth with his neighbour: for we are members one of another. Be ye angry, and sin not: let not the sun go down upon your wrath: Neither give place to the devil. Let him that stole steal no more: but rather let him labour, working with his hands the thing which is good, that he may have to give to him that needeth. Let no corrupt communication proceed out of your mouth, but that which is good to the use of edifying, that it may minister grace unto the hearers. And grieve not the holy Spirit of God, whereby ye are sealed unto the day of redemption. Let all bitterness, and wrath, and anger, and clamour, and evil speaking, be put away from you, with all malice: And be ye kind one to another, tenderhearted, forgiving one another, even as God for Christ's sake hath forgiven you." —Ephesians 4:20-32,

"Be ye therefore followers of God, as dear children; And walk in love, as Christ also hath loved us, and hath given himself for us an offering and a sacrifice to God for a sweetsmelling savour." —Ephesians 5:1-2

BIBLICAL REFLECTIONS

I Timothy 5:4—*"But if any widow have children or nephews, let them learn first to shew piety at home, and to requite their parents: for that is good and acceptable before God."*

Colossians 3:8—*"But now ye also put off all these; anger, wrath, malice, blasphemy, filthy communication out of your mouth."*

REFLECTIVE EXERCISE
Change Unhealthy Patterns of Family Interaction

Examine the relationships in your family and identify factors that determined how you responded.

_____
_____
_____

Examine the scripture in the above text—Ephesians 4:22-5:2—and identify the patterns of thinking and behaving that were passed down to you.

_____
_____
_____

What behavior would you like to see changed in your life?

_____
_____
_____

Setting Healthy Boundaries

As stated above, healthy boundaries help people feel secure. What healthy boundaries were set in your family to provide for your safety and security?

_____
_____
_____

Identify what you would like to change about your family beliefs, values, behaviors, thoughts, rituals, and roles to provide more protection and freedom for your loved ones.

_____
_____
_____

FREE FROM FEAR

"I sought the LORD, and he heard me, and delivered me from all my fears." —Psalm 34:4

Fear is not of God. Fear comes from a lie the enemy has spoken into your life. Human babies aren't like baby animals who instinctively respond to their environment. Animals are up and walking and feeding within hours of birth. Children born of humans have everything in their DNA that they need to grow and develop, but as we learned through the Development Stages, everything is synchronized according to God's plan written in that DNA. God established a family, which includes a set of parents, whom God designed to provide protection and safety as well as to provide for children's needs as they grow and develop mentally and physically and develop the capacity of caring for themselves. As we know, children do not communicate until they are nearly two years of age, and parents must learn to interpret their needs by the sounds they make and help the child learn to verbalize their needs.

When there are no parents, absent parents, or parents who do not know how to parent, the children's needs are neglected, and children are abandoned to care for themselves physically and emotionally. The family, as we will learn later, is a key factor in the development of a child's view of himself, his world, and his God. When these needs aren't met, the child is stressed and cries, and in his way tries to meet his own needs. When that fails, fears and distrust in his world begin to formulate fears in his mind which then begins to cause physiological, emotional, and even mental issues that can't be resolved because they can't speak.

SAFE AND UNSAFE PLACES

"Preserve me, O God: for in thee do I put my trust." —Psalm 16:1

Conflicts and stressful situations are a part of everyday life. In any relationship, two or more people may disagree because they have different goals, ideas, or needs. Conflict is often difficult for people to handle because it produces anxiety and fear. For people to have healthy relationships, they need to develop healthy life skills that will help them resolve conflicts in a nonviolent manner.

These skills are learned from early childhood if the environment is conducive to growing and learning. The following are homes that are typically unsafe for children:
- Homes where the mother or father abuse physically, emotionally, or mentally.
- Homes where drugs and alcohol rule rather than love and discipline.
- Homes that are so rigid and stifling that children can't speak.
- Homes where no one takes responsibility and where chaos reigns, rather than order.
- Homes where lying/deceiving/breaking promises predominate, and trust can't grow.
- Homes so filled with anger that loves and trust can't survive.

Some of the qualities you would want to provide and nurture in your home or church, or you would look for in childcare facilities, are the following:

QUALITIES OF SAFE PLACES:
1. Basic needs are met.
2. Love is freely given and received.
3. The opportunity is given to grow toward maturity.
4. Trust abounds.
5. People are free to serve one another.
6. Emotions are expressed freely.
7. Relationships are strong and healthy.

QUALITIES OF UNSAFE PLACES
1. Leaders are dictatorial and unaccountable.
2. Abuses remain unrecognized and not acknowledged.
3. People are in pain.
4. People are blamed and shamed.
5. Those who give in to the sick are "insiders", those who see and speak the truth is "outsiders."
6. Punishment for noncompliance is severe.
7. People are manipulated.
8. The abusive leaders keep things secret.
9. Followers "walk on eggshells".
10. Followers believe whatever the leader tells them.

REFLECTIVE EXERCISE
Safe and Unsafe Places

As stated earlier in the lesson about the *Family Tree*, the family is one of the greatest influences on how we form the choices we make as individuals. The impact of all the information gathered from our culture put pressure on the family system. This "culture pressure" will either strengthen or weaken the family and thus affect the family's effectiveness in the molding of individuals.

Questions to ask yourself regarding your environment

Am I safe here? Do I fit in here? Can I be myself here and survive? What do I have to contribute to this world?

_____
_____
_____

Name a Safe Place you feel free to visit to find peace and joy:

_____
_____
_____

Name a place where you feel unsafe:

_____
_____
_____

✝

BIBLICAL REFLECTIONS
"As for God, his way is perfect; the word of the LORD is tried: he is a buckler to all them that trust in him." —II Samuel 22:31

PRAYER TO CHANGE UNHEALTHY FAMILY RELATIONSHIPS

Dear Lord,

I want my family to honor You and bless You. I repent that I have not set a godly example for my spouse and my children to imitate. I know that I have grieved You in many of my attitudes and ways. I desire to be a Christ-like example for my family. I repent of (name the family interactions to stop) I lift this up to You, Father, in Jesus' name. Amen

Lesson Fourteen

BREAKING FREE

Lesson Fourteen

Breaking Free

"Wherefore say unto the children of Israel, I am the LORD, and I will bring you out from under the burdens of the Egyptians, and I will rid you out of their bondage, and I will redeem you with a stretched out arm, and with great judgments:" —Exodus 6:6

GUIDE TO SPIRITUAL SURGERY

"Behold, I will bring it health and cure, and I will cure them, and will reveal unto them the abundance of peace and truth." —Jeremiah 33:6

Just as a doctor does testing and examinations to understand a problem before determining what actions he will take—as a caregiver, we must be careful not to jump to quick conclusions about a problem. If we are dealing with a cut finger, it is not difficult to conclude that we need an antiseptic and a Band-Aid. However, for deeper cuts and wounds, we may need to take the injured person to an emergency room for stitches.

Similarly, the longer-lasting and more persistent a psychological problem, the more research it may take to discover the root cause of the symptoms. First, it is important to identify the symptoms. The stated problem may be migraine headaches, depression, problems at work, or marital difficulties. In former times when towns were smaller and had intergenerational families, everyone knew our parents, grandparents, and every child. They knew everyone's family profile, character, and history. Pastors were at the same church for years, so they knew about everyone in the family. It was their duty to baptize, marry, and bury generations of families and their relatives. A pastor could quickly determine the root of a problem. However, today when those resources aren't available, and a problem is deeply hidden, it may take other means to discern the root cause of the symptoms such as a *Personal Inventory Questioner*, which can be found at the end of this book.

Once generational patterns and cycles that characterize the family have been identified, we will look for underlying beliefs and issues that need to be addressed. In this section, we will address several necessary steps to receive total healing. It is most important to realize that any hope for healing will depend upon us, and whether or not we use the power and authority given to us through our relationship with Jesus Christ.

There are several steps in the process of healing. Do not worry about taking the steps in order. The Lord will lead us through the process as we become ready spiritually. He won't give us more than we can handle.

Below, are steps provided by God through the shed blood of Jesus Christ through which all healing takes place. There is no formula with some exceptions; it does not matter which comes first or last. Some steps would need to be in order. For instance, to know what to forgive you must first confess; to know what to bind and loose, we must be aware of the strongholds and be ready to let go. Standing on God's promises is something we do throughout the process of sanctification. Deliverance takes place as we repent and forgive.

The necessary steps include the following:
1. Renouncing all oaths, vows, and inner vows ("I never" or "I will never")
2. Severing unhealthy emotional, physical, sexual, and spiritual bonds
3. Repentance of ways you have sinned (even if you were innocent or ignorant)
4. Forgiveness of those who have hurt or offended us (even yourself)
5. Cleansing and purification
6. Renouncing any ties to cults, occult, witchcraft, and other cult or occult practices
7. Renewing of the mind, body, and spirit
8. Deliverance

REFLECTIVE EXERCISE
Guide to Spiritual Surgery

Review your responses to the exercises in previous chapters to prepare for your "surgery." What did you learn from your responses? Note your revelations below.

Can you identify your fruit as illustrated in the Tree of Bondage vs. Tree of Freedom?

_____
_____
_____

What did you learn from your Genogram?

_____
_____
_____

Can you identify a developmental stage in your life that would indicate a developmental scar? If so, what was the event and how did it affect you?

_____
_____
_____

What lies have you believed?

_____
_____
_____

FASTING

Old Testament fasting was used as an expression of sorrow over sin or a plea asking God to physically deliver His people from disaster. One example of this type of fasting can be found in the book of *Esther*. When the annihilation of the Israelites was planned, they fasted as a plea asking God to protect them—(Esther 4:16). In the book of *Joel*, fasting was also used during the severe drought which left thousands of people dead—(Joel 1:14). In Chapter 58 of the book of *Isaiah*, God addresses the fact that fasting had degenerated into a "purely religious" exercise, as practiced by the legalistic Pharisees. God instructed the Israelites that they were to use fasting and prayer in order to loose the bands of wickedness, to undo the heavy burdens, and to let the oppressed go free, and that ye break every yoke?

> *"Is not this the fast that I have chosen? to loose the bands of wickedness, to undo the heavy burdens, and to let the oppressed go free, and that ye break every yoke? Is it not to deal thy bread to the hungry, and that thou bring the poor that are cast out to thy house? when thou seest the naked, that thou cover him; and that thou hide not thyself from thine own flesh?* —Isaiah 58:6-7

Additional scriptures that address fasting are:
- Daniel calls for a fast to repent for the nation's sins. "*O Lord, hear; O Lord, forgive; O Lord, hearken and do; defer not, for thine own sake, O my God: for thy city and thy people are called by thy name.*" —Daniel 9:19
- People were told in Matthew to fast but not "to make a show of it" but "to do it privately." "*Moreover when ye fast, be not, as the hypocrites, of a sad countenance: for they disfigure their faces, that they may appear unto men to fast. Verily I say unto you, They have their reward.*" —Matthew 6:16
- Jesus responded to the disciples regarding a young boy who had a demon but was unsuccessful in their deliverance. Upon questioning Jesus, He responded to them. "*Howbeit this kind goeth not out but by prayer and fasting.*" —Matthew 17:21

WAITING ON THE LORD

If we will pray and ask, God will answer. Often, we rush into prayer without considering how God would have us pray. We are told in Psalm 27:14, *"Wait on the LORD: be of good courage, and he shall strengthen thine heart: wait, I say, on the LORD."*

In Acts, we find that the disciples waited upon the Lord (Acts 1:14) and talks about the disciples waiting to hear the Lord speak. (Acts 13:1-4)

LISTENING TO THE SPIRIT IN PRAYER

Little Samuel had to learn that the voice he heard calling him was from God.—I Samuel 3:10

In Isaiah 30:21 Samuel said, *"And thine ears shall hear a word behind thee, saying, This is the way, walk ye in it, when ye turn to the right hand, and when ye turn to the left."*

> *"And the times of this ignorance God winked at; but now commandeth all men every where to repent:"* —Acts 17:30

Very few people understand the healing power of repentance today, because society has done away with sin. If we do not recognize our sin, we have no need to repent. We are told by non-believers there is no "right or wrong," and that all is relative. Our sins are considered mistakes, diseases, genetic flaws, or dependent upon how one interprets the Word. Sin is acceptable—even *popular*!

- If a lie will keep me from hurting another's feelings, then that's better than the truth.
- If going along with the crowd to humiliate and intimidate someone will keep me from looking like a coward, then it's okay.
- If aborting a baby keeps me from having to face disappointing Mom and Dad or keeps me from being embarrassed in front of my friends, then it's the better thing to do.
- If sleeping with a partner to avoid taking responsibility for myself, or to meet a temporary need for sex and companionship, it is no sin.
- If lying about my past gets me the job, there is no sin.

Lying, according to a study by Josh McDowell (*Right from Wrong*, Word Publishing, 1994) makes us more popular. This could only be true in a truth-deprived society. The heart is deceitful above all things and beyond cure. According to the prophet Jeremiah, *"The heart is deceitful above all things, and desperately wicked: who can know it?"*—Jeremiah 17:9

We have been taught not to take sin seriously, everybody does it and there is no penalty to pay. Sin invades every part of our nature and personality—our minds, will, affection, conscience, disposition, and imagination. Notice the list includes thoughts, words, and actions. This shows that, in God's sight, all sin is equally serious. Some of us think of sin as only serious acts such as murder, robbery, drugs, alcohol abuse, rape, etc., but the Bible "pulls no punches" and goes right to the point (root). If we hold on to hate, unforgiveness, rebellion, and disobedience, then we are holding sin in our hearts.

> ***Sin is everything that fails to meet God's perfect standards...***
> **OUR LANGUAGE, OUR ATTITUDES, OUR EMOTIONS, OUR ACTIONS, OUR THOUGHTS.**

Sin is ... anything that fails to meet God's perfect standards. Anything we think, say, or do that does not line up with God's will is missing the mark God has set for us to bring joy and prosperity to our lives. Those of us who do not know God or His Word believe these sins are freedoms, rather than slavery, and don't even see the need to be set free from evil ways. We think that by receiving Jesus Christ as Savior and Lord of our lives, we are going to have to give up all our "freedoms."

Have you received Jesus Christ as your Savior? You can choose to live in sin and slavery and suffer the consequences of eternal separation from God, or you can receive Him and His salvation and be set free from the sinful nature that rules you.

Even our defiance and unwillingness to accept His Word as truth is a sin. The Bible teaches that sin is lawlessness, deliberate rebellion against God's authority and law. No civil law forces us to lie, cheat, have impure thoughts, or sin in any other way. If we choose to sin, we choose to break God's holy law, and there are consequences to that.

BIBLICAL REFLECTIONS
Repentance

Jeremiah 15:19—*"Therefore thus saith the LORD, If thou return, then will I bring thee again, and thou shalt stand before me: and if thou take forth the precious from the vile, thou shalt be as my mouth: let them return unto thee; but return not thou unto them."*

Psalm 32:1-7—*"Blessed is he whose transgression is forgiven, whose sin is covered. Blessed is the man unto whom the LORD imputeth not iniquity, and in whose spirit there is no guile. When I kept silence, my bones waxed old through my roaring all the day long. For day and night thy hand was heavy upon me: my moisture is turned into the drought of summer. Selah. I acknowledged my sin unto thee, and mine iniquity have I not hid. I said, I will confess my transgressions unto the LORD; and thou forgavest the iniquity of my sin. Selah. 6 For this shall every one that is godly pray unto thee in a time when thou mayest be found: surely in the floods of great waters they shall not come nigh unto him. Thou art my hiding place; thou shalt preserve me from trouble; thou shalt compass me about with songs of deliverance. Selah."*

REFLECTIVE EXERCISE
Repentance

You just learned that sin is anything that fails to meet God's perfect standards. Yes, also our defiance and unwillingness to accept His Word as truth is a sin. Review the *Biblical Reflections* listed above and understand how important repentance is to God.

Write your understanding of the repentance scriptures.

_____
_____
_____

Look at your own life considering these scriptures. For what sins do you feel the need for repentance?

_____
_____
_____

Go before the Lord and repent of your sins and make a new covenant with the Lord to walk in righteousness.

Prayer for Personal Repentance

Father God,
I realize I am a sinner at heart and there is no way that I can be forgiven without repentance, a turning away from my sinful ways. I truly desire to be forgiven. Therefore, I repent of my sins(s) of ____(identify)____ and I ask your Holy Spirit to teach me your ways that I may not grieve You and Your Holy Spirit. In Jesus Christ's name. Amen.

> **"And the times of this ignorance God winked at;
> but now commandeth all men every where to repent:"** Acts 17:30

FORGIVING OTHERS

*"Blessed is he whose transgression is forgiven, whose sin is covered.
Blessed is the man unto whom the LORD imputeth not iniquity, and in whose spirit there is no guile."* —Psalm 32:1-2

Today, seeking forgiveness from God is rarely mentioned, yet every sin grieves the heart of God. We are told in Isaiah 63:10, *"But they rebelled, and vexed his holy Spirit: therefore he was turned to be their enemy, and he fought against them."*

Sometimes our own sin brings upon us the wrath of God. Yet for those of us who repent and seek forgiveness, He is quick to forgive. In our culture, forgiveness is man to man—but every sin against man is a sin against God and must be brought to the throne of Grace to receive God's forgiveness

"Whose soever sins ye remit, they are remitted unto them; and whose soever sins ye retain, they are retained." —John 20:23

If we hold unforgiveness, it will block our blessings from God. Forgiveness is a powerful thing. Our unforgiveness can keep another person in bondage with us. Any relationship that is broken keeps people in bondage to one another until such time as forgiveness takes place. The state of unforgiveness allows the spirit of strife, revenge, resentment, hate, and many other spirits to abide in us. This also hinders the healing of the other person because it does not allow the woundedness in the other person to heal. The person we are angry with may not even be aware of our anger. There are times God will use one person to bring healing to many people just through repentance and forgiveness.

Forgiveness is a powerful thing.
Forgiveness is a choice.
Forgiving does not necessarily mean that we are going to forget.
Forgiving is not pretending that the offense didn't matter.
Forgiving doesn't necessarily mean the person is entirely off the hook.
<u>**UNFORGIVENESS**</u> in your heart is committing emotional suicide.

Steps of Forgiveness:

1. Line your will up with God's will. Purpose in your heart to work the process through—regardless of the pain and fear.
2. Ask the Holy Spirit to shed His light into your soul to reveal the roots of the bitterness in your heart.
3. Be specific about what it is you need to forgive.
4. Identify your response to the offense.
5. Be honest before God regarding how you feel about the person or the event.
6. Forgive the offense.
7. Pray and ask God to forgive you for holding the unforgiveness in your heart.

8. Identify any inner vows you have made regarding your offender and renounce them.
9. Renew your mind with the Word of God.
10. Forgive yourself for your part and pray for healing.
11. Identify any area in which you are blaming God.
12. Release God, others, and yourself from any false or unrealistic expectations you may have had for them.
13. Forgive God. Ask Him to show you what He was trying to work into your spirit.
14. Pray for the person you have forgiven.

BIBLICAL REFLECTIONS
Forgiveness

Psalm 32:2—*"Blessed is the man unto whom the LORD imputeth not iniquity, and in whose spirit there is no guile."*

Luke 23:34—*"Then said Jesus, Father, forgive them; for they know not what they do. And they parted his raiment, and cast lots."*

Romans 5:8—*"But God commendeth his love toward us, in that, while we were yet sinners, Christ died for us."*

Ephesians 4:31-32—*"Let all bitterness, and wrath, and anger, and clamour, and evil speaking, be put away from you, with all malice: And be ye kind one to another, tenderhearted, forgiving one another, even as God for Christ's sake hath forgiven you."*

Colossians 3:13—*"Forbearing one another, and forgiving one another, if any man have a quarrel against any: even as Christ forgave you, so also do ye."*

REFLECTIVE EXERCISE
Forgiveness

Review again the list of five (5) items that describe forgiveness. See page 116. In your own words, describe what you understand to be the benefits of forgiveness.

_____
_____
_____
_____
_____

Think of someone you need to forgive.

Is there anything you need to forgive yourself for?

Review the Steps to Forgiveness (pages 116–117) listed in this section and identify persons you are holding something against and make a list. Take the list of names and go through the above steps given to identify what you need to do. Take personal time with God and lift these persons in prayer to release them from the power of your unforgiveness and release them to God for His justice to be done.

Prayer of Forgiveness

Dear God,

I know I have sinned against _____(name)_____ for offending him/her (or holding unforgiveness towards him for his/her offense towards me). I am having a hard time forgiving them because it still hurts. Your Word tells me I won't be forgiven unless I forgive others. I know I have sinned and fallen short of Your glory. Please forgive me for my offense against them. I was angry/bitter regarding (what angered you). Though I knew it was wrong, I allowed this to grow in my heart, bringing separation from my brother/sister as well as from You.

Father, speak Your truth to me and renew my mind with Your Word. I don't want to harbor bitterness/revenge anymore, nor do I want to blame others. With your help, I take full responsibility for changing this situation.

Forgive me, God, and release (name) from the unrealistic expectation I have had for them. I also release myself from all the unrealistic expectations I have had for myself. I pray for your Holy Spirit to intercede to break every stronghold of bitterness and strife between us and I renounce every lie the enemy has told me. I choose to believe that You can bring good from this situation. I place my anger/bitterness in Your hands and trust You to bring justice and peace where I have failed.

Thank you, Father, for sending Jesus to make it possible for me to be released from this heavy burden. Amen.

RENOUNCING TIES TO CULTS, OCCULT, AND WITCHCRAFT

*"Regard not them that have familiar spirits, neither seek after wizards,
to be defiled by them: I am the LORD your God."* —Leviticus 19:31

In our culture today, many active cults and occult groups are prevalent at all levels of society. We would be shocked to know how many influential people practice the "dark arts" and worship gods introduced through other religions and New Age practices. As of 1985, a district court in Virginia declared that under the US Constitution, *Wicca* is to be considered an official religion. As such, the United States Armed Forces ensures that a chaplain for the *Wicca Religion* must be provided for the military forces. In the mid-1900s, Satanism was also made an official "religion" and given a non-profit status in America.

The *Personal Inventory Questionnaire* can be used to discover who may have been involved in a cult, the occult, or have dabbled in the supernatural, psychic phenomenon, Spiritualism, or new age systems of belief. Whatever we may have bonded with through vows or by making oaths to their gods, philosophies, or ideologies, can put us in bondage to those beliefs.

Receiving our total healing through Christ means we must divorce ourselves from these foreign or false gods and covenant with our Savior, Jesus Christ, so we can follow Him and His precepts. This will require a "breaking away" or the severing of bondages to those ways that are foreign to Christianity and renounced by God Himself.

We will need to examine our own history and identify every area of involvement which needs to be renounced (i.e., playing sorcery games, tarot card reading, consulting with mediums, Ouija Boards, etc.). If we are going to be pure vessels that God can use, we must repent of "seeking answers" from false gods, renounce the activity, and break any ties to our soul—as a result of what God would call idolatry.

Isaiah 8:19 states, *"And when they shall say unto you, Seek unto them that have familiar spirits, and unto wizards that peep, and that mutter: should not a people seek unto their God? for the living to the dead?"* Another biblical reference to this is in II Kings 23:24 where we are told, *"Josiah got rid of the mediums and spiritists, … and the other detestable things … This he did to fulfill the requirements of the law written in the book that Hilkiah the priest had discovered in the temple of the Lord."*

Remember, we aren't just dealing with flesh and blood, but with evil principalities. Therefore, do not take the privilege of prayer lightly. Prayer is spiritual warfare with spiritual principalities.

> **The key to inner healing is knowing principles of healing so when the Holy Spirit moves you to bind, loose, repent, forgive or stand; you will know what He means.**

REFLECTIVE EXERCISE
Renouncing Ties to Cults, Occult, and Witchcraft

Considering your own history, identify every area of involvement that must be renounced. If we are going to be pure vessels God can use, we must repent of seeking answers from false gods. We must renounce the activity along with any ties or bondage to our soul as a result of what God would call idolatry.

Before we do any of this work it is important to follow the steps of spiritual preparation and protection. We will also use the prayers used in *Chapter One* to take us through this process of cleansing and sanctification.

The following scriptures will also help us prepare for this time of Spiritual Warfare. Remember, our weapons aren't the world's weapons of warfare, but are His weapons used to tear down strongholds in the spirit realm.

STANDING ON THE PROMISES
Psalm 46:1—*"God is our refuge and strength, a very present help in trouble."*

Proverbs 18:10—*"The name of the LORD is a strong tower: the righteous runneth into it, and is safe."*

Jeremiah 33:3—*"Call unto me, and I will answer thee, and shew thee great and mighty things, which thou knowest not."*

LISTENING TO THE SPIRIT IN PRAYER
Isaiah 30:21—*"And thine ears shall hear a word behind thee, saying, This is the way, walk ye in it, when ye turn to the right hand, and when ye turn to the left."*

Isaiah 50:4—*"The Lord GOD hath given me the tongue of the learned, that I should know how to speak a word in season to him that is weary: he wakeneth morning by morning, he wakeneth mine ear to hear as the learned."*

Habakkuk 2:1—*"I will stand upon my watch, and set me upon the tower, and will watch to see what he will say unto me, and what I shall answer when I am reproved."*

Revelation 2:7—*"He that hath an ear, let him hear what the Spirit saith unto the churches; To him that overcometh will I give to eat of the tree of life, which is in the midst of the paradise of God."*

PROTECTION THROUGH PRAYER

Psalm 3:3—*"But thou, O LORD, art a shield for me; my glory, and the lifter up of mine head."*

Psalm 91:9-15—*"Because thou hast made the LORD, which is my refuge, even the most High, thy habitation; There shall no evil befall thee, neither shall any plague come nigh thy dwelling. For he shall give his angels charge over thee, to keep thee in all thy ways. They shall bear thee up in their hands, lest thou dash thy foot against a stone. Thou shalt tread upon the lion and adder: the young lion and the dragon shalt thou trample under feet. Because he hath set his love upon me, therefore will I deliver him: I will set him on high, because he hath known my name. He shall call upon me, and I will answer him: I will be with him in trouble; I will deliver him, and honour him."*

Psalm 5:11- *"But let all those that put their trust in thee rejoice: let them ever shout for joy, because thou defendest them: let them also that love thy name be joyful in thee."*

Prayer to Renounce Cult and Occult Involvement

Dear Heavenly Father,

I desire truth in my inner self and facing this truth is the way of liberation. I acknowledge that I have been deceived by the father of lies and that I have deceived myself. By faith, I have received You into my life and I am now seated with Christ in the heavenlies. I acknowledge that I have the responsibility and authority to resist the devil, and when I do, He will flee from me.

I reject and disown all sins of my ancestors and renounce all demonic oaths or vows spoken over me or passed on to me by my ancestors. As one who has been crucified and raised with Jesus Christ, I renounce all Satanic assignments that are directed toward me and my family. I announce to Satan and all his forces that Christ became a curse for me when He died on the cross. I reject any and every way in which Satan may claim ownership of me. I belong to the Lord Jesus Christ Who purchased me with His own blood. I reject all other blood sacrifices whereby Satan may claim ownership of me. I declare myself to be eternally and completely signed over and committed to the Lord Jesus Christ. By the authority I have in Jesus Christ, I command every familiar spirit and every enemy of the Lord Jesus Christ that is in or around me to leave my presence forever. I commit myself to my Heavenly Father, and to do His will from this day forward. In Jesus' name. Amen.

Lesson Fifteen
RENEWING THE MIND

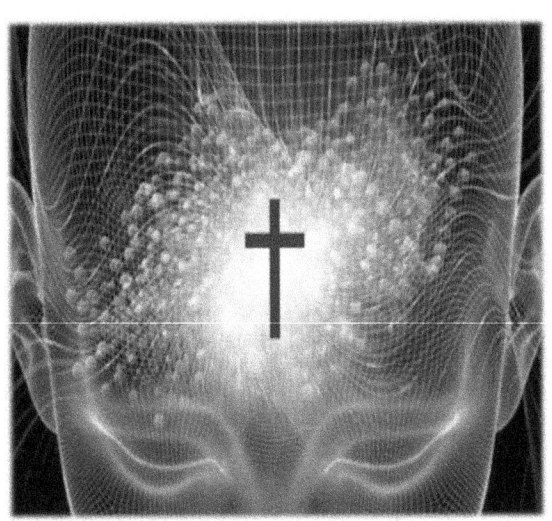

Lesson Fifteen

Renewing the Mind

"And be not conformed to this world: but be ye transformed by the renewing of your mind, that ye may prove what is that good, and acceptable, and perfect, will of God." —Romans 12:2

The mind is the playground of the enemy. Each of us is born in the image of God, with His DNA, a potential of health and wholeness, and a knowing of right and wrong. When working with sexual abuse victims, we rarely meet victims of abuse who didn't know that what was being done to them was wrong. It stirred something in them that told them it was wrong, just as surely as it was hurtful. Yet often because what is being said or done is by an adult, one in whom their very survival exists, the inner knowing is defiled, and the knowledge of truth is twisted. With regular conditioning or programming by philosophies, attitudes, and beliefs that are predominant around them, they can quickly begin to believe the lie over the truth. We are told, that in the latter times, *"For many shall come in my name, saying, I am Christ, and shall deceive many. And when ye shall hear of wars and rumors of wars, be ye not troubled: for such things must needs to be; but the end shall not be yet."*—Mark 13:6-7

MIND RENEWAL

The greatest task of recovering the truth is to begin by identifying the lies we have believed. Once we have been made aware of God's truth, we have a gauge for measuring what is a lie and what is truth. God's Word is the Spirit of Truth, and God Himself is TRUTH. Mind renewal means transforming those lies into truth so we can walk in the freedom and peace that truth brings.

> **WHAT MIND RENEWAL IS NOT:**
> - Positive thinking
> - Cognitive therapy
> - Transcendental meditation
> - Hypnosis
> - Guided imagery
> - Self-driven (humanistic)

WHAT MIND RENEWAL IS:	ENEMIES OF RENEWAL:
• Spirit driven • Dwelling on God's will • Divine revelation • Thinking like Christ • Instantaneous • Complete • Genuine	• A busy schedule • A negative mood • Bitterness • Selfishness • Worldliness • Ungodly companions • Anger • Fatigue

Recovery shouldn't be understood as the removal or changing of the memory, but rather the reinterpretation of the memory by replacing the embedded lie with the truth. Jesus knows all things and will shed His light upon the lie to disengage it and replace it with the truth.

Shame and guilt are merely the emotions that match the belief we embrace. This is how the enemy keeps us in bondage to sin—by continually accusing us and bringing condemnation upon us. Consider Romans 8:1-2, *"There is therefore now no condemnation to them which are in Christ Jesus, who walk not after the flesh, but after the Spirit. For the law of the Spirit of life in Christ Jesus hath made me free from the law of sin and death."*

EMBRACING TRUTH

Sometimes we may know the truth but can't embrace it. Other lies may be keeping us from the ability or the desire to grasp that which we can't logically agree. As we present our pain to God, He will reveal the source of that pain as well as the accompanying lie(s). As He reveals those lies and changes the lie to truth, the truth sets us free. Once we hear the truth from God, it empowers us to move on with our lives. Galatians 5:1 says: *"Stand fast therefore in the liberty wherewith Christ hath made us free, and be not entangled again with the yoke of bondage."*

The enemy loves to keep God's children in slavery to him. Shame and guilt are his major weapons. But as Galatians 4:3-5 tells us, *"Even so we, when we were children, were in bondage under the elements of the world: But when the fulness of the time has come, God sent forth his Son, made of a woman, made under the law, To redeem them that were under the law, that we might receive the adoption of sons."*

BIBLICAL REFLECTIONS

II Corinthians 10:3-5—*"For though we walk in the flesh, we do not war after the flesh: (For the weapons of our warfare are not carnal, but mighty through God to the pulling down of strong holds;) Casting down imaginations, and every high thing that exalteth itself against the knowledge of God, and bringing into captivity every thought to the obedience of Christ;"*

Romans 12:2—*"And be not conformed to this world: but be ye transformed by the renewing of your mind, that ye may prove what is that good, and acceptable, and perfect, will of God."*

John 8:31-32—*"Then said Jesus to those Jews which believed on him, If ye continue in my word, then are ye my disciples indeed; And ye shall know the truth, and the truth shall make you free."*

Hebrews 9:14—*"How much more shall the blood of Christ, who through the eternal Spirit offered himself without spot to God, purge your conscience from dead works to serve the living God?"*

I Peter 5:8-9—*"Be sober, be vigilant; because your adversary the devil, as a roaring lion, walketh about, seeking whom he may devour: Whom resist stedfast in the faith, knowing that the same afflictions are accomplished in your brethren that are in the world."*

REFLECTIVE EXERCISE
RENEWING THE MIND

You learned earlier that the mind is the playground of the enemy. In addition, you know that the greatest task of healing and recovery is the identification of the lies you have believed. Ask the Lord to renew your mind and replace the lies with the truth. Review the two lists on *What Mind Renewal is Not* and *What Mind Renewal Is* (pgs.123–124).

Study the scriptures regarding renewing the mind about faulty thoughts and beliefs that are listed in the *Biblical Reflections* in this chapter. Pick two scriptures (a list of which scriptures you are using) and write your understanding of renewing the mind.

_____
_____
_____
_____

REFLECTIVE EXERCISE
POWER OF LIES

As we realize the power of lies over our minds and emotions and the resulting choices in behavior to protect ourselves from further pain, we recognized how the enemy's lies were intended to confuse and defeat us. By seeking God's truth regarding the lies, God is able to dispel the lie and take away the power it has over our lives. *Remember, the enemy does not stop lying to us but when we learn to discern the lies from God's truth, he will no longer be able to hinder us from being all God wants us to be!* The point is to listen to God's truth; either through His voice or through His Word (the Bible). If we want to receive advice from a friend, we must sit down and talk to Him. Jesus is our friend, and if we take timeshare our problems with Him, He will reveal His truth to us. Taking time to let Him show us the truth takes personal time with Him. If you are ready to try the process of renewing the mind, you may follow the following steps:
- Identify an emotion that creates problems for you.
- Let the emotion reveal the type of situation that caused this emotion.

- Ask the Lord to show you what your mind is saying that has created these emotions (remember, it is the thought that causes the pain, not the event). Allow yourself to get in touch with the situational memory that created the emotion for the first time.
- Allow the memory to replay itself. Now, look at the memory in light of how you saw it as a child. Since Jesus was there, ask HIM to show you what He saw, allow Him to show you what happened, and give you understanding.
- Let the Lord show you the lie you believed that is embedded in the memory.
- Let the Lord show you how this lie has affected your life.
- This memory may cause a similar memory to enter your thoughts to reveal a similar situation where the same lie is embedded.
- Ask the Lord to show you the biblical truth (God's perception).
- His Word will help you reframe this event and release you from the power of the lie you believed.

You may want to make notes regarding the memory, the lie that was embedded in the memory, and how the lie affected your view of yourself.

_____
_____
_____
_____

> **Remember, each time God reveals a lie and speaks the Truth about it, the lie is dispelled, and the emotional pain is healed. If more pain exists, that is a sign, more than one lie is involved. Repeat the steps until all the pain is gone and you have complete peace with it.**

DYING TO SELF

"Stand fast therefore in the liberty wherewith Christ hath made us free, and be not entangled again with the yoke of bondage." —Galatians 5:1

Sin and pain cause us to focus on self. Matthew 24:12 states, *"And because iniquity shall abound, the love of many shall wax cold."* When we have a toothache, we don't pay much attention to anybody else's pain. A reflection of this truth is found in I Samuel with King Saul.

"Then he said, I have sinned: yet honour me now, I pray thee, before the elders of my people, and before Israel, and turn again with me, that I may worship the LORD thy God." —I Samuel 15:30

Saul had sinned and thought only of how he was going to look in front of his people. He wanted to hide and cover up his sin with "fig leaves" of pride. The Biblical Reflections at the end of this section speak to the need for dying to sin so that new life may be released.

As we read in the previous section, Paul tells us in I Corinthians 13 to put away childish ways but when we are bound by the lies, it is difficult to let go. We may repent, forgive, and confess the truth of God's Word, but when similar situations present themselves, those lies seem to have more power than the truth. This happens because we have not allowed the lie to be totally dispelled by the truth. Many times, we try to do it ourselves by simply memorizing the Word of God, but we never let the Word get down into our hearts. Sometimes it takes breaking free from our environment to be able to see the truth as God sees the truth. We may have to give up old friends, old ways, and/or old habits before we can get the truth into our hearts. Surrounding ourselves with people who trust God, whose habits are healthy, honest, and loving is essential. We must begin to experience the truth of God's Word before we can trust it. This is dying to self, dying to our old ways of thinking, feeling, and doing.

> *"Then they took away the stone from the place where the dead was laid. And Jesus lifted up his eyes, and said, Father, I thank thee that thou hast heard me. And I knew that thou hearest me always: but because of the people which stand by I said it, that they may believe that thou hast sent me. And when he thus had spoken, he cried with a loud voice, Lazarus, come forth. And he that was dead came forth, bound hand and foot with graveclothes: and his face was bound about with a napkin. Jesus saith unto them, Loose him, and let him go."* —John 11:41- 44

When Lazarus came forth from the tomb, the preceding scripture tells us his hands and feet were wrapped as well as a cloth was wrapped around his face. Jesus stated to the people assembled *"Loose him and let him go."* How would we have liked to have had the job of unwrapping those strips of cloth from his once decaying body? Our sins are like the dead, decaying flesh of Lazarus.

Some people who come to us will be like dead men walking. They come to us with "messy bindings" that must be removed for them to live, move and breathe. They, like the dead bones mentioned earlier, may have life in them, but the sinews, the muscles, and the tissues are all decaying. With God's healing touch, the sinews, muscles, and skin are replaced and made healthy. Then the individual receives Christ and His Holy Spirit, and his life takes on a "new" life through Christ. We are the ones to whom Jesus hands these people. Jesus says, "loose him"—meaning, take off the bindings. The bindings for us represent the lies, deceptions, old faulty beliefs, destructive habits, and wounds caused by past pain and sin. As these are removed and replaced by discipline, faithfully abiding in the Word and the power of Jesus, the old self is laid down and the "new" life in Christ takes place.

An alcoholic who is converted by receiving Christ into his life may make a total conversion from sin to serving God, but he may have a family still feeling the pain from the wounds of his past neglect and abuse. There may be habits and faulty beliefs that need to be transformed by the Word of God. When converted, we receive Christ and His Spirit in us. His blood, His very life, flows through us. That is the beginning of our sanctification. It is not an event, but sanctification is a process of Christ going through our whole lives, cleansing, purifying, and renewing us so that we can walk in the truth and light of His Word and in the power of His Spirit.

WE MUST RECOGNIZE THAT JUST BECAUSE A PERSON HAS EXPERIENCED CONVERSION (BEEN RAISED FROM THE DEAD) IT DOES NOT ALWAYS MEAN HE HAS BEEN TOTALLY HEALED AND SET FREE FROM HIS OLD LIFE.

BIBLICAL REFLECTIONS

Romans 8:5—*"For they that are after the flesh do mind the things of the flesh; but they that are after the Spirit the things of the Spirit."*

Romans: 8:1-2—*"There is therefore now no condemnation to them which are in Christ Jesus, who walk not after the flesh, but after the Spirit. For the law of the Spirit of life in Christ Jesus hath made me free from the law of sin and death."*

Acts 1:8—*"But ye shall receive power, after that the Holy Ghost is come upon you...."*

Galatians 5:1—*"Stand fast therefore in the liberty wherewith Christ hath made us free, and be not entangled again with the yoke of bondage."*

REFLECTIVE EXERCISE
DYING TO SELF

Study the scriptures listed above and below to understand the concept of **DYING TO SELF**. Understand that though Christ died for our sins, the enemy of our soul is constantly trying to tempt us to remain in our sins or to return to our old sinful ways. This section will help you recognize that once we receive Christ into our lives, we have the power of His Holy Spirit to guide and strengthen us in our walk of faith.

"Then he said, I have sinned: yet honour me now, I pray thee, before the elders of my people, and before Israel, and turn again with me, that I may worship the LORD thy God." —I Samuel 15:30

How is Saul trying to solve his sin problem?

_____
_____

"And when he thus had spoken, he cried with a loud voice, Lazarus, come forth. And he that was dead came forth, bound hand and foot with graveclothes: and his face was bound about with a napkin. Jesus saith unto them, Loose him, and let him go." —John 11:43-44

How does Lazarus' rising from the dead relate to our own bondage?

_____
_____

Identify the "bindings" that must be removed to be totally free of the old self.

_____
_____

If grave clothes represented the covered, hidden sin(s) and Jesus said to the people "Remove his grave clothes," what would need to be removed to set you free?

_____
_____

(You may pray this prayer over every sin or hindering force the Lord shows you)

PRAYER FOR DYING TO SELF

Dear Lord,
You demonstrated through Lazarus's life that we can die to the old and be reborn. I confess that there are many things I say, do, and believe that bring death to my body daily. I desire to "die" to those old ways that hinder my walk with You. I recognize (name of sin or habit) in my life that keeps me from being like Christ. Lord, unwrap this binding from me that I may be free. You shed Your blood for my sin, and I claim the authority in the name of Jesus to be free from this dead flesh. I cast it off in the name of Jesus. I pray that the power of my flesh may decrease that He may increase, and I may be more alive in Christ. Amen.

TRANSFORMING

"And be not conformed to this world: but be ye transformed by the renewing of your mind, that ye may prove what is that good, and acceptable, and perfect, will of God." —Romans 12:2

Once people go through the healing process, they assume they are finished. However, when a person comes out of surgery, is he healed? Just because a person has a cast on his leg, is it healed? When an alcoholic stops drinking is he healed? No! There is much repair to be done to rebuild their life in a healthy way.

When a person has a stroke that paralyzes his legs and is healed, he still has to re-train his muscles. The stroke patient will attend therapy classes for months after a stroke to learn to walk again. Physical therapy teaches the muscles how to function properly and builds them up through repetitive exercises. In the same way, those of us who have had mental or emotional disturbances lived a life of inappropriate behavior, or experienced abuse all our lives won't get healed and immediately begin to live peacefully, act appropriately, or feel free. The process of renewing our self-image involves capturing and living a new sense of self and learning to respond to the world in new ways.

REFLECTIVE EXERCISE
Restoring Your Sense of Identity

Read the following scriptures (next page) in the *Who Am I In Christ* chart and make notes on your personal revelation(s) from God regarding guidance in learning and restoring your identity:

_____
_____
_____
_____

WHO AM I IN CHRIST?

Ephesians 1:4, 11-14 He chose me, predestined me, redeemed me.
I Corinthians 15:45-49 I bear likeness to earthly man and heavenly man, body and spirit
Jeremiah 1:5 He formed me in the womb.
Romans 8:14-17 I am a son of GOD, heir of GOD, co-heir with CHRIST
2 Corinthians 5:17 In CHRIST, I am a new creation.
Romans 9:10-13 In the womb; GOD's choice
Isaiah 49:1-4 GOD formed me to be His servant.
Ephesians 1:3-7 GOD chose me, predestined me, redeemed me, forgave me, sealed me, gave me a guaranteed inheritance.
Mark 9:23 All things are possible for him who believes.
Romans 8:37-39 A conqueror through CHRIST, nothing can separate me from His love.
Leviticus 19:2 Be holy, because I, the Lord your GOD, am holy.
Deuteronomy 7:6 GOD has chosen you to be His chosen people.
Deuteronomy 14:2 GOD has chosen you to be His treasured possession.

CHANGING FAULTY BELIEFS AND BEHAVIORS

"And you, that were sometime alienated and enemies in your mind by wicked works,
yet now hath he reconciled" —Colossians 1:21

We must be conscious of inappropriate or dysfunctional behavior before we can even know we need to change. Therefore, those of us who are rebuilding our lives need to be taught, mentored, and disciplined in the appropriate thing to do or say. For example, many of us who were victims of abuse have never felt we had the right to speak up and let our needs be met. Some practice and experience will be necessary for us to grow and mature in that area. It is important that we have a safe place to learn how to do that. Just as the stroke patient goes to the physical therapist who knows what needs to be done, we who are being healed from emotional or mental illness may need to be in a safe place with safe people to learn new ways of living our lives before we can interact with our families, especially if the family was part of their abuse.

The following are four (4) steps in the process of replacing faulty beliefs and behaviors:

1. We must become consciously aware of our faulty thoughts and behaviors.
   (To recognize our thoughts and behaviors)
2. We must make a conscious plan to change our faulty thoughts and behavior.
   (Have a plan of "how" we are going to change)
3. We must consciously change our thoughts and behavior.
   (We must "think" about what we say and do)
4. Through conscious practice, our conscious change becomes unconscious
   (We perform the new behavior without thinking)

FIND A SAFE PLACE TO TRY NEW BEHAVIOR

We need to be with people who are safe and who can help us identify normal and abnormal behavior. Some of us have never seen normal behavior or normal attitudes. By watching healed people handle situations and listening to them work through problems, we can learn. This is how children learn, by watching and listening to their parents. We are needing a lot of encouragement and renewing of our minds because the enemy does not give up his territory without a fight.

In addition to being with safe people, we need people that are also honest and patient and who will persevere and encourage us as we learn to walk in the power of the Holy Spirit.

REFLECTIVE EXERCISE
Changing Faulty Beliefs and Behaviors

Reflect on the four (4) steps listed above that must take place for change to become effective in your life.

- Take one example of a faulty thought or behavior and "plan" how you will consciously change that thought or behavior. (Examples of thought/behavior—"I can't cook" or "When I am bored, I eat.")
- Identify how you would "choose" to change your thinking or behavior. (Example—"I'm going to learn how to fry an egg", "I am going to take a walk, visit someone instead of eating")
- State when you will begin this plan. Make notes of your success.
- Not happy with how you are living your life? Think of a person who would be a good mentor. A good mentor would be one who would be honest and patient as well as encouraging and persevering in holding you accountable for your changes. It is a must that the mentor be a person with whom you would feel safe.

EXAMINE BEHAVIORAL PROBLEMS

"Examine me, O LORD, and prove me; try my reins and my heart." —Psalm 26:2

The Word of God is the only measure we have for right and wrong. If we examine our behavior considering what the world believes is right or wrong, it will only cause us to measure ourselves against another human being.

Once we have given our life to Christ, however, it is very important to perform an inventory of our life and what we have done with it. It is time to set our heart on things above and to separate ourselves from those things that will turn our hearts away from our desired goal. There are many examples of people who did or didn't follow God's laws, such as sowing and reaping and reaping the consequences of what had been sown.

Note to Remember: <u>THE ENTIRE BIBLE IS OUR GUIDE TO LIVING!</u>

The Word tells us in Colossians 3:5-10 to: *"Mortify therefore your members which are upon the earth; fornication, uncleanness, inordinate affection, evil concupiscence, and covetousness, which is idolatry: For which things' sake the wrath of God cometh on the children of disobedience: In the which ye also walked some time, when ye lived in them. But now ye also put off all these; anger, wrath, malice, blasphemy, filthy communication out of your mouth. Lie not one to another, seeing that ye have put off the old man with his deeds; And have put on the new man, which is renewed in knowledge after the image of him that created him:"*

Paul continues, "Put on therefore, as the elect of God, holy and beloved, bowels of mercies, kindness, humbleness of mind, meekness, longsuffering; Forbearing one another, and forgiving one another, if any man have a quarrel against any: even as Christ forgave you, so also do ye. And above all these things put on charity, which is the bond of perfectness. And let the peace of God rule in your hearts, to the which also ye are called in one body; and be ye thankful. Let the word of Christ dwell in you richly in all wisdom; teaching and admonishing one another in psalms and hymns and spiritual songs, singing with grace in your hearts to the Lord. And whatsoever ye do in word or deed, do all in the name of the Lord Jesus, giving thanks to God and the Father by him."—Colossians 3:12-17

All of scripture is designed to help us align our lives with God's will for us. We will find God ever present to help us examine our hearts, minds, and actions. He will guide us through this process of sanctification.

BIBLICAL REFLECTIONS

II Corinthians 13:5—*"Examine yourselves, whether ye be in the faith; prove your selves. Know ye not your own selves, how that Jesus Christ is in you, except ye be reprobates?"*

Jeremiah 17:10—*"I the LORD search the heart, I try the reins, even to give every man according to his ways, and according to the fruit of his doings."*

Psalm 11:4—*"The Lord is in his holy temple; the Lord is on his heavenly throne. He observes the sons of men; his eyes examine them."*

God expects us to change our behaviors after we have received His Holy Spirit. In fact, He sends the Holy Spirit to help us change. Review the Biblical Reflections scriptures to see how we are to change.

Read the scriptures Colossians 3:5-17, in the previous text. Note your understanding of behavior problems.

_____
_____
_____
_____

What are the behavior problems you want to change to be more like Christ?

_____
_____
_____

PRAYER TO CHANGE BEHAVIORAL PROBLEMS

Dear Lord,
I confess that I have participated in wrong and evil behaviors that are offensive in your sight. Thank You that You have already made provision for my forgiveness by Your shed blood on the cross. I repent of my sins of (name each sinful behavior)

_____

_____

_____

_____

_____

I am truly sorry for those I have hurt and offended in the process, but I mainly repent that I have offended You. I choose not to walk in that way again. Father, I submit my will to You that You may, through Christ, line my will up with Yours, for You abide in me and I in You. I am Yours now and I draw upon Your strength, Lord, to fulfill my commitment to lead a life worthy of all You have done for me. I give You permission to show me other sinful behaviors I am not now fully aware of. In the flesh, I am weak. But in You, I am strong, I ask this in Jesus' name. Amen.

EXPERIENCING FREEDOM

You have experienced many milestones during these weeks we have been together, becoming prepared spiritually for personal inner healing, ministry to others, growing in your understanding of Your authority in Christ, learning the importance of discipline, and practicing the process of sanctification. You have listened to others' stories and shared Your own. In a sense, you have become family with others in this class.

It is important as we bring this class to an end for you to reflect on the process of healing that you have experienced; the oaths, vows, and bondages released, the sins repented, the unresolved hurts healed, the lies revealed and the walls you have laid down in the process of dying to self. It is our prayer that by using the Bible studies, the assessment tools which provided windows to the soul, you would continue to process your pain and search for the lies of the enemy as well as the truth that sets you free.

PROTECTION AGAINST THE ENEMY

> *"Because he hath set his love upon me, therefore will I deliver him:*
> *I will set him on high, because he hath known my name."* —Psalm 91:14

Once we are brought to healing and begin the process of restoration, we must not be left defenseless. We must, as we heal and restore, learn how to use the same steps that we used for our own healing process to help others heal. We must learn to turn to Christ for our solutions rather than creating a dependence on another person. Other people can't always be there for us, but God can. We must claim the power we have in Jesus Christ and use it so that when we are amid a problem, we will know God's solution is only a prayer away. The steps we use for our healing are the same that we will be using for the seekers who come to us for hope and healing. The same authority that we have for healing is the same authority that we have for our protection and those around us.

> **HE HAS PROMISED US PROTECTION. WE STAND ON THE PROMISES OF GOD. HIS WORD IS TRUTH. WE MUST DAILY BE AWARE OF OUR AUTHORITY AND HOW TO USE THE "WEAPONS" HE HAS PROVIDED FOR US.**

PRAYER FOR HEALING AND RESTORATION

Dear Heavenly Father,

I thank You for all You have taught and shown me throughout this course of study. I am eternally grateful to You for the many scriptures and biblical principles in this course that have shed light on my life. I pray that my growth and healing will continue as I invite You to reveal any faulty beliefs or unbelief in me that block my relationship with You, and my brothers and sisters. Help me see any behaviors that would bring disrepute to the name of Christ or bring shame to my church or family. I desire to live according to Your Word, and to bless and honor You, Jesus, my Lord and Savior.

Lord, I desire to love You with all my heart, soul, and mind. Please teach me to love my neighbor as myself and help me to change any unhealthy interactions with people so I can love my family as my mission field here on earth. I pray for Your protection and guidance as I go from here to do battle for the Kingdom of God where You plant me. I open myself to Your teachings and directives so that I may go and multiply the Kingdom of God through my words and actions. May I always glorify You in all I do and speak. In Jesus' Name. Amen.

".... forgetting those things which are behind, and reaching forth unto those things which are before, I press toward the mark for the prize of the high calling of God in Christ Jesus." —Philippians 3:13-14

Hope and Healing

Reference Notes

LESSON ONE—CHANGING TIMES

Pg. 2—<u>Sexual Behavior in the Human Male, Sexual Behavior in Human</u> Female by Alfred C. Kinsey. Wardell B. Pomeroy, Clyde E. Martin, Paul H. Gebhard and W. B. Saunders, Philadelphia, (1953©).

Pgs. 2–4—Kinsey, Sex and Fraud, by Dr. Judith A. Reisman, Edward Eichel, Huntington House Publishers, 1990.

Pg. 3—Evolution teachings, Harvard Law School, Christopher Columbus Langdell, President of Harvard Univ., Charles W. Eliot…concept led to Darwin's theory of evolution which led to secular humanism. 1870–1960s—sex education in the USA.

Pg. 4—Family Households Pew Research Center analysis of AU.S. Census Bureau data. (2017)—Children living with solo mom Pew Research Center Census data.

Pg. 5—<u>Effects</u> on our children—Statistics about Children from single-parent homes. (U.S. Centers for Disease Control)—(CDC) and the Guttmacher Institute.—Abortion).

Pg. 5—Epidemic of Suicide—Centers for Disease Control and Prevention (CDC) WISQARS Leading Causes of Death Reports in 2016. Suicidal Thoughts and Behaviors Among U.S. Adults 2016—Courtesy of SAMHSA.

Pg. 7—Mental Health Facts by Mental Health America

Pg. 7—Drug Abuse and Addiction reports by National Institute on Drug Abuse

Pg. 8—Pornography by United Families.org.

LESSON TWO: WHERE THE BATTLE BEGAN

Pgs. 10–11—FUTURE WAR OF THE CHURCH by Chuck D. Pierce and Rebeca Wagner Systema

Pgs. 11–12—Principalities Over Families (Commentary made available by http://www.answersIngenesisorg/creation/v20/13/china.asp© 2005 Answers in Genesis)

Pg. 15—Equipping for Warfare—

Pgs. 15–17—Receiving the Holy Spirit

Pg. 17—Know God's Word

Pgs. 18–20—Wear the Armor of God

LESSON THREE—TREE OF BONDAGE VS. TREE OF FREEDOM

Pgs. 22–23—GETTING TO THE ROOT—Book: "A Child Called "It" by Dave Pelzer (Health Communications, Inc., Deerfield Beach, Fla., ©1995 (1)

Pg. 23—Born Only Once, intra-womb bonding—copyright by Dr. Conrad Barrs, M.D.

Pg. 24—ICA Theory (Inclusion+ Control + Affect) Design by Proctor & Gamble for a personal Growth and Development Training event, 1970's (Millie McCarty)

Pg. 25—<u>Tree of Bondage vs. Tree of Freedom</u>—diagram—source unknown

LESSON FOUR—FAMILY SYSTEMS—LAYING THE FOUNDATIONS

Pgs. 27–31—Family Systems Model—Best reference: Bowen Family Systems Theory materials. My material came from my workshop notes from a training class for Human Growth & Development Training by Procter-Gamble Industry, 1975–76.

LESSON FIVE—FAMILIES MAKE A DIFFERENCE

Pgs. 33-34—FOUR BASIC TYPES OF FAMILIES—from conference notes 1980s. Best resource: Bowen Family Systems Theory, Peter Titleman, Ph.D. © 1990)

LESSON SIX—GROWING UP IN STAGES

Pg. 38—Other Altars, Craig Lockwood, pages 231–232, How trauma affects the developmental stages of the brain).
Pg. 39—Alan Shores, Professor at UCLA—Developing Core Self-Bonding, brain image studies in relation to ADHD and ADD.
Pg. 39—Jean Illsley-Clarke and Connie Dawson, authors of Growing Up Again, Hazelden Education, ©1989.
Pg. 41—Child Development Chart (Erikson + Erikson & Clarke Combined charts. Source: Growing Up Again by Clarke and Connie Dawson, Hazelden Educ. © 1992. Servant Publications

LESSON SEVEN—TAKING THE AX TO THE ROOT

Pg. 46—Generational Sins—Deuteronomy 5: 9-10 (Holy Bible)
Pg. 47—*Ten Commandments*—Deuteronomy 5:6-21, Exodus 20: 1-17,
Pgs. 48–49—Blessings and Curses—Deuteronomy 28:1—68
Pgs. 50–56—THE GENOGRAM– Best resource: Genograms in Family Assessment by Monica McGoldrick & Randy Gerson, Norton Publishing, ©1985.

LESSON EIGHT—WALLS WE BUILD

Pgs. 58–59—Nietzsche—pathological narcissism—1960's–1970's (Madison 721@aol.com, AOL Friedrich Nietzsche—Existentialism, www.age-of-the-sage.org/philosophy/nietzsche.html).
Pgs. 61–64—COMMON DEFENSE MECHANISMS—Protecting the Self: Defense Mechanisms in Action by Phoebe Cramer, Ph.D. ©2002
Pg. 64—The Lies We Believe by Dr. Chris Thurman, Thomas Nelson, Copyright, © 2002

LESSON NINE—WEB OF LIES

Pg. 68—Sowing and Reaping—Matthew 12:33, Galatians 6:7-9 Proverbs 19:5, Hosea 10:12
Pg. 69—The Lies We Believe by Dr. Chris Thurman, Thomas Nelson, Copyright, © 2002
Pg. 72—GOD'S PERCEPTION VS. MY PERCEPTION—unknown source
Pgs. 70–71—"*Other Altars*" by Craig Lockwood, Compcare Publishers, 1993.
Pg. 73—MEMORIES HOLD LIES—Ishbane's Conspiracy by Randy Alcorn

LESSON TEN – LIES, OATHS, AND VOWS
Pgs. 76–78—LIES, OATHS, AND VOWS—Holy Bible: James 3:4-6, 10 RENOUNCING OATHS AND VOWS: Holy Bible: Hosea 10:4, Psalm 6:1-5, Matthew 5:33

Pgs. 78–81—INNER VOWS—PROMISES WE MAKE WITH OURSELVES—Holy Bible: Job 22-27, Psalm 51:6, Isaiah 19:21, Proverbs 20-25.

LESSON ELEVEN—OUT OF DARKNESS
Pg. 83—Johari Window—Developed by Joseph Luft and Harry Ingham, 1955 www.copmmunicationskills/johariwindow-model

Pg. 84—Diagram—Neuron activity in the Hippocampus (Internet Source Unknown)

Pg. 84—Drawing of Prefrontal Cortex, the Hippocampus and Lymbic System and their functions. (Internet Source Unknown)

Pg. 86—Cycle of Dysfunction—Adapted by Millie McCarty from the Cycle of Sin and Addiction– by Patrick Carnes, Out of the Shadows, Understanding Sexual Addiction, ©1994, Net Library, Inc.

Pgs 87–88—Defense Mechanisms—Multiple Domains of Impairment

Pg. 88—System Damage & Disempowered

Pg. 91—CYCLE OF ILLUMINATION

LESSON TWELVE—CYCLE OF SIN & ADDICTION
Pgs. 95–96—The Iceberg Theory—Hidden Evidence of unresolved conflict

Pgs. 97–99—Cycle of Sin and Addiction Cyclical Terms—Out of the Shadows, Understanding Sexual Addiction, By Patrick Carnes, ©1994, Net Library, Inc.

Pgs. 97–99—CYCLE OF SIN AND ADDICTION—Adapted from Out of the Shadows, Understanding Sexual Addiction, By Patrick Carnes, ©1994, Net Library, Inc.

Pgs. 101–102—Sin Leads to Sickness and Death—Psalm 32:1-5

LESSON THIRTEEN—HEALTHY BOUNDARIES
Pgs. 104–105—Drs. Henry Cloud and John Townsend, authors of Healthy Boundaries, 1992 ©Zondervan

Pg. 105—Loving ways to create safe relationships

Pg. 105—Change Unhealthy Patterns of Family Interaction

Pg. 108—Qualities of Safe and Unsafe Places

LESSON FOURTEEN—BREAKING FREE
Pg. 114—Repentance—Josh McDowell (Right from Wrong, Word Publishing, ©1994

Pgs. 116–117—FORGIVING OTHERS—Total Forgiveness by R. T. Kendall, ©2002, Charisma House

Pg. 118—"Quote" (Source Unknown)

Pgs. 119–121—Renouncing Cults, Occult, Witchcraft

LESSON FIFTEEN—RENEWING THE MIND

Pgs. 123–124—Renewing the Mind—What it is and What it is NOT.

Pgs. 124—Embracing Truth Exercise—POWER OF LIES

Pgs. 125–126—NINE STEPS TO RENEWING THE MIND

Pgs. 126–127—Dying to Self

Pgs. 129–130—Dying to Self and Transforming the Mind—Biblical Teachings

Pgs. 130–131—Changing Faulty Beliefs and Behaviors—Find a Safe Place to Try New Behavior

Pgs. 133–134—Protection Against the Enemy—Psalm 91:14—Prayer for Healing and Restoration

PERSONAL INVENTORY QUESTIONNAIRE

In order to look more closely at our families and develop our *genogram*, a tool used to identify patterns (positive and/or negative) that may have been passed down from generation to generation, this questionnaire is helpful as a probe into the past and an examination of your current life status in multiple areas. Many people have forgotten some of the details of their growing-up years—this tool asks probing questions to help you remember things you may have forgotten over time. It is also quite useful for anyone in the helping profession who has been or could be helpful to you in this journey. It provides an overall picture of who you are and where you have come from in a relatively short amount of time.

Name _____

Age _____ Sex _____ Birthplace _____

Current Marital Status _____

Education (Highest Grade Completed) _____

Are You Currently Employed and/or Going to School? If so, Where? _____

List Anything Significant About Your Current or Past Work or School Experience.
_____
_____
_____
_____

FAMILY HISTORY

Were you raised by anyone other than your parents? _____

If So, Explain _____

Are you Adopted? _____

How many children in your childhood family? _____
Where are you in your family line of siblings? _____

Relationship to father during childhood.	GOOD	BAD	INDIFFERENT
Relationship to mother during childhood.	GOOD	BAD	INDIFFERENT
Relationship to siblings during childhood.	GOOD	BAD	INDIFFERENT

Has there significant change in any of these relationships? Please explain.

_____
_____
_____
_____

Please circle your answer:

Father	Living	Deceased	Unknown
Mother	Living	Deceased	Unknown
Sibling	Living	Deceased	Unknown
Sibling	Living	Deceased	Unknown
Sibling	Living	Deceased	Unknown
Sibling	Living	Deceased	Unknown

What of the following did you experience during your childhood?

- Broken home
- Removed from home
- Unhappy childhood
- Loneliness
- Excessive fear
- Night terrors
- Stammering
- Bed wetting
- Nail biting
- Sleep walking
- Physical disabilities
- Learning disabilities
- Other learning problems
- Molestation
- Sexual encounters incest
- Frequent illnesses
- Serious illnesses

Parents Marital Status:

Married…How many years? _____

Separated…How old were you? _____

Divorced…How old were you? _____

Never Married

Widowed

Relationship: Good   Bad   Indifferent

Parent's Remarriage: Please explain any important information regarding your parent's marital history.

_____
_____
_____
_____

Parents Religious Background:

Father: _____

Mother: _____

Stepparents: _____

General health of your parents and siblings growing up and currently:

_____
_____
_____
_____

Did your parents wish you were of the opposite sex? _____

In your opinion, did your parents wish you had never been born? _____

How many children do you have? _____

Ages and names:

_____
_____

What is your current relationship with your children? _____
_____

With whom are you now living? _____

Does your name have any particular significance as to family tradition or cultural or national heritage?

_____
_____
_____

What nationality or cultural/ethnic group do you must identify with?

What was the work and economic status of your family growing up?

Think about your family and friends. Identify how you feel when you are around them. Circle your answer.

    INCLUDED vs. EXCLUDED
    VISIBLE AND NEEDED vs. INVISIBLE AND INADEQUATE
    FREE TO EXPRESS FEELINGS AND IDEAS or HINDERED
    LIKE A LEADER vs. A FOLLOWER
    LIFE OF THE PARTY vs. PARTY POOPER
    LOVED AND ACCEPTED vs. UNLOVED AND UNACCEPTED
    FEELING OF BELONGING vs. AN OUTSIDER

Identify where your parents and siblings fit in relation to the love you feel FROM and FOR them—how close or far away were they to you while growing up? Place them on this chart where you would place them relative to how close you felt to them or how closely they related to you.

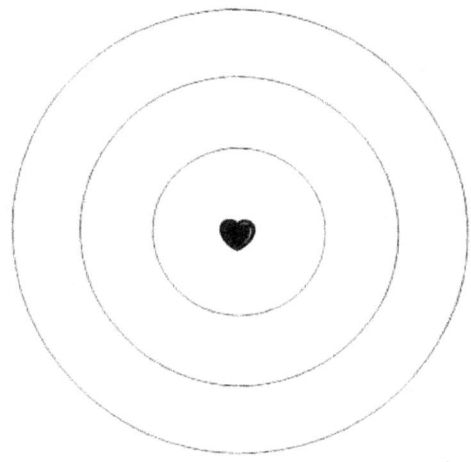

RELIGIOUS AND SPIRITUAL HISTORY

Church affiliation: Present: _____ Past: _____

Are you a born-again believer? _____ When were you saved? _____

Water Baptized? _____ If so, what age? _____

How often do you currently attend church? _____

Do you have regular devotions in the Bible? _____

Do you find prayer difficult? _____

Have there been any contacts or involvement in your personal life or family history with areas such as occults, middle eastern or new age religions, paganism, consulting with mediums or psychics, tarot card, palm or horoscope readings, the conjuring of spirits, black or white magic or any other activity or practice that would be considered spiritual or religious groups or cults? If YES, please explain. These are areas that may have impacted you on a deeper spiritual level than you realize and are important to recognize if there were any harmful doors opened in your life.

_____
_____
_____
_____
_____
_____
_____
_____
_____

MENTAL, EMOTIONAL AND TRAUMA HISTORY

Have there been any major traumas in your life?

_____
_____
_____
_____
_____
_____
_____

Which of the following have you struggled with or had difficulty controlling?

Doubts	Depression
Chronic Pain	Obsessive thoughts
PMS	Hatred
Anger	Daydreaming
Anxiety	Blasphemous thoughts
Insecurity	Fear of death
Worthlessness	Fear of losing mind
Fantasy	Fear of suicide
Compulsive thoughts	Fear of hurting loved ones
Dizziness	Frustration
Headaches	Lustful though
Loneliness	

MORAL CLIMATE

During the first 18 years of your life, how would you rate the moral atmosphere in which you were raised?

Morals	Overly Permissive	Permissive	Average	Strict	Overly Strict
Clothing	1	2	3	4	5
Sex	1	2	3	4	5
Dating	1	2	3	4	5
Movies	1	2	3	4	5
Literature	1	2	3	4	5
Free Will	1	2	3	4	5
Drinking	1	2	3	4	5
Smoking	1	2	3	4	5
Church Attendance	1	2	3	4	5

Did you have a keen interest in sex before puberty? _____

Have you looked at pornography? _____

If so, how often? _____

MEDICAL HISTORY

Have you ever had any medical surgeries? _____
If so, for what reason and at what age?
_____
_____

Have there been medical traumas and/or hospitalization?
_____
_____

Have you had an abortion? _____
If so, when? _____
Have you had a miscarriage? _____
If so, when? _____
Diagnosed with PMS? _____
Hospitalization for emotional illness? _____
Why? _____
Currently under the care of a doctor? _____
A psychiatrist? _____
On drug therapy? _____
Please explain _____
Subject to depression? _____
Frequency/Duration of Depression _____
Any other significant medical concerns or history that has greatly impacted your life?
_____
_____
_____

Do you have any addictions or cravings that you find difficult to control? (Sweets, drugs, alcohol, tobacco, food, etc.) _____
_____

Are you an alcoholic? _____
If so, for how long? _____
Have you ever used street drugs? _____
If so, for how long? _____
If drug and alcohol free, how long have you been in recovery? _____
Are you presently using drugs or alcohol? _____
Have you ever misused prescription drugs? _____
If so, for how long? _____
Are you still using them? _____
Explain any history of drug or alcohol use or abuse within your family that has directly affected your life.
_____
_____
_____

PERSONAL/MISC.

Do you listen to music regularly? _____

What type do you enjoy most? _____

How many hours of TV do you watch per week? _____

Are you a veteran of any foreign wars? _____

If so, which one(s)? _____

Is there any part of your life (a large block of time) that you don't remember?
_____
_____

Have you done any foreign travel? _____ If so, where? _____
_____

General hobbies, likes, and interests:
_____
_____

Any other significant information pertaining to your life in the past or present:
_____
_____
_____
_____

OTHER BOOKS WRITTEN BY MILLIE McCARTY

PATHWAYS TO HOPE AND HEALING **(Copyright 2008) Published by Ambris Publishing**
    WORKBOOK
    POWERPOINT PRESENTATION
    TEACHER'S GUIDE
    MENTOR TRAINING SYLLABUS
    PHH PROMO POWERPOINTDVD—TEACHINGS OF NINE BASIC PRINCIPLES (3 DVDs)
    DVD—Entire PHH book 8 DVDs

PHH for PATHFINDERS (Resource workbook for rehabilitation of survivors of abuse & trauma).

PATHWAYS TO HOPE AND HEALING FOR CHILDCARE WORKERS
PHH—WORKBOOK FOR CHILDREN & YOUTH (3 age groups) **(Copyright 2004)**

WHY WE CAN'T "JUST GET OVER IT" **(Copyright 2007) Published by Ambris Publishing**
    WORKBOOK

PHH for SMALL GROUP MINISTRY (Trauma-based interactive lessons using biblical principles and proven professional assessment tools) focus SPRUCE (Systematic Process for Resolving Unresolved Conflict Eternally). Recommended for professional counselors working with people with mental/emotional problems, addictions, obsessions, etc.

PATHWAYS TO HOPE AND HEALING FOR CHILDCARE WORKERS
    PHH—WORKBOOK FOR CHILDREN & YOUTH (3 age groups) (Copyright 2004)

WHY WE CAN'T "JUST GET OVER IT" (Copyright 2007) Published by Ambris Publishing
    STUDENT WORKBOOK
    POWERPOINT PRESENTATION
    MENTOR TRAINING SYLLABUS
    VIDEO OF CLASS PRESENTATION
    VIDEO CLIPS FROM MOVIES

TRAUMA RECOVERY TRAINING **(Copyright 2013)**
(Combination of JUST GET OVER IT and PATHWAYS TO HOPE AND HEALING).
    WORKBOOK
    POWERPOINT PRESENTATION
    OPEN BOOK EXAMS
    TRAINING SYLLABUS
    MENTOR TRAINING SYLLABUS
    TEACHER TRAINING (PHH, JGO & TRT)

POWERPOINT TEACHING OF ENTIRE BOOK
TEN-HOUR INTRO TO TRT

<u>RUTH: SECRETS OF THE SILENCED VOICES—CASE STUDY</u> (Copyright 2012)
<u>RUTH: SECRETS OF THE SILENCED VOICES</u>—A GUIDE TO WORKING WITH PEOPLE WITH DISSOCIATIVE IDENTITY DISORDERS—CHILD SEXUAL TRAUMA,
<u>SYLLABUS</u> 48 hour class (LESSON PLANS)
<u>STUDENT ACTIVITY BOOK</u>
<u>POETRY ANTHOLOGY</u> by RUTH—(Separate book—for students only)
<u>PRAYER—PATHWAY OF LIFE</u>—WORKBOOK—COPYRIGHT (2002)
<u>SEXUAL ABUSE SMALL GROUP TRAINING GUIDE</u>: Putting Together the Shattered Pieces of Your Life
<u>SEXUAL ABUSE TRAINING MANUAL</u>—COPYRIGHT
<u>THE PATHFINDER</u>—Written & Copyrighted for Lighthouse Counseling Services
<u>MAN CUT DOWN TREE WITHOUT KNOWING WHY</u> by KELTIE—Copyrighted by Lighthouse Counseling Services.

Your thoughts and perceptions can keep you in bondage!!!!!

Systematic Process of Resolving Unresolved Conflict Eternally

SPRUCE

Provides faith-based processes and
Proven psychological assessment tools that

"Get to the root" of the problem

and "Resolves the mental conflict!"

Millie McCarty, M.A., LPCC, Author, Pastor, Trainer, CEO

International Institute for Trauma Recovery 2023

REFRENCES LIST

- Sexual Behavior in the Human Male, Sexual Behavior in Human Female by Alfred C. Kinsey. Wardell B. Pomeroy, Clyde E. Martin, Paul H. Gebhard and W. B. Saunders, Philadelphia, (1953©).
- Kinsey, Sex and Fraud, by Dr. Judith A. Reisman, Edward Eichel, Huntington House Publishers, 1990.
- Harvard Law School, Christopher Columbus Langdell,
- President of Harvard Univ., Charles W. Eliot…concept led to Darwin's theory of evolution which led to secular humanism. 1870–1960s—sex education in the USA.
- Pew Research Center analysis of A U.S. Census Bureau data. (2017)—Children living with solo mom Pew Research Center Census data.
- Statistics about Children from single-parent homes. (U.S. Centers for Disease Control)- (CDC) and the Guttmacher Institute.—Abortion).
- Centers for Disease Control and Prevention (CDC) WISQARS Leading Causes of Death Reports in 2016. Suicidal Thoughts and Behaviors Among U.S. Adults 2016—Courtesy of SAMHSA.
- Mental Health Facts by Mental Health America
- Drug Abuse and Addiction reports by National Institute on Drug Abuse
- Pornography by United Families.org.
- FUTURE WAR OF THE CHURCH by Chuck D. Pierce and Rebeca Wagner Systema
- Principalities Over Families (Commentary made available by http://www.answersIngenesisorg/creation/v20/13/china.asp© 2005 Answers in Genesis)
- "A Child Called "It" by Dave Pelzer (Health Communications, Inc., Deerfield Beach, Fla., ©1995 (1)
- Born Only Once, intra-womb bonding- copyright by Dr. Conrad Barrs, M.D.
- ICA Theory (Inclusion+ Control + Affect) Design by Proctor & Gamble for Personal Growth and Development Training event, 1970's (Millie McCarty)
- Tree of Bondage vs. Tree of Freedom—diagram—source unknown
- Family Systems Model—Best reference: Bowen Family Systems Theory materials. My material came from my workshop notes from a training class for Human Growth & Development Training by Procter-Gamble Industry, 1975–76.
- Family Systems Model—Best reference: Bowen Family Systems Theory materials. My material came from my workshop notes from a training class for Human Growth & Development Training by Procter-Gamble Industry, 1975–76.
- FOUR BASIC TYPES OF FAMILIES—from conference notes 1980s. Best resource: Bowen Family Systems Theory, Peter Titleman, Ph.D. © 1990)
- Other Altars, Craig Lockwood, pages 231–232, How trauma affects the developmental stages of the brain).
- Alan Shores, Professor at UCLA—Developing Core Self-Bonding, brain image studies in relation to ADHD and ADD.
- Jean Illsley -Clarke and Connie Dawson, authors of Growing Up Again, Hazelden Education, ©1989.
- Child Development Chart (Erikson + Erikson & Clarke Combined charts. Source: Growing Up Again by Clarke and Connie Dawson, Hazelden Educ. © 1992. Servant Publications

- THE GENOGRAM—Best resource: Genograms in Family Assessment by Monica McGoldrick & Randy Gerson, Norton Publishing, ©1985.
- (Madison 721@aol.com, AOL Friedrich Nietzsche—Existentialism, www.age-of-the-sage.org/philosophy/nietzsche.html)
- Protecting the Self: Defense Mechanisms in Action by Phoebe Cramer, Ph.D. ©2002
- The Lies We Believe by Dr. Chris Thurman, Thomas Nelson, Copyright, © 2002
- GOD'S PERCEPTION VS. MY PERCEPTION—unknown source
- "*Other Altars*" by Craig Lockwood, Compcare Publishers, 1993
- Ishbane's Conspiracy by Randy Alcorn
- Johari Window—Developed by Joseph Luft and Harry Ingham, 1955
  www.copmmunicationskills/johariwindow-model
- Diagram—Neuron activity in the Hippocampus (Internet Source Unknown)
- Drawing of Prefrontal Cortex, the Hippocampus and Lymbic System and their functions. (Internet Source Unknown)
- Cycle of Dysfunction—Adapted by Millie McCarty from the Cycle of Sin and Addiction– by Patrick Carnes, Out of the Shadows, Understanding Sexual Addiction, ©1994, Net Library, Inc.
- The Iceberg Theory—Hidden Evidence of unresolved conflict Internet Source—What is the Iceberg theory?—Embrace yourself, embrace the world (embrace-yourself-embrace-the-world.com)
- Cycle of Sin and Addiction Cyclical Terms—Out of the Shadows, Understanding Sexual Addiction, By Patrick Carnes, ©1994, Net Library, Inc.
- CYCLE OF SIN AND ADDICTION CHART—Adapted from Out of the Shadows, Understanding Sexual Addiction, By Patrick Carnes, ©1994, Net Library, Inc.
- Drs. Henry Cloud and John Townsend, authors of Healthy Boundaries, 1992 ©Zondervan
- Josh McDowell (Right from Wrong, Word Publishing, ©1994
- Total Forgiveness by R. T. Kendall, ©2002, Charisma House
- "Saying" (Source Unknown)
- All scriptures are taken from the King James Version of the bible

www.ingramcontent.com/pod-product-compliance
Lightning Source LLC
Chambersburg PA
CBHW081157020426
42333CB00020B/2541